GETTING OVER GROWING OLDER

How to Change Your Life by Staying Positive

Brigitte Nioche

The strategies and suggestions in this book are based on the author's experiences; the opinions expressed are her own, and the information provided is for general purposes only and is not meant to substitute for advice a reader might seek from a physician or other health care professional.

Published by:
Brigitte Nioche
New York, NY

ISBN: 978-0-692-62385-5

Cartoons reprinted by permission:

© Robert Weber/The New Yorker Collection/The Cartoon Bank. Pages 5, 81, 90, 95, 111, 122, 169, and 201

© Marisa Acocella Marchetto/The NewYorker Collection/The Cartoon Bank. Page 115

© Donald Reilly/The New Yorker Collection/The Cartoon Bank. Page 42

© Ed Fisher/The New Yorker Collection/The Cartoon Bank. Page 26

Cover photo: Manny Parks
Cover and interior design: Gary A. Rosenberg

For all the women in the world
Because women make the world a better place

Joy and Peace

I want to live a simple life
A life in joy and peace
A life with work, and song, and play
My spirit free, at ease
A life in love with every bird
And every flower too
A life of reaching out my arms
Embracing all of you
I want to live a simple life
A life in joy and peace
A life with work, and song, and play
In solitude, but not alone
My spirit free at ease.

Written by Alice O'Connor for her friends when she was eighty-two years old.

Contents

Introduction

I never think of my age, and I don't think I am old. The calendar says otherwise, but what the calendar says has no affect on how I feel or look.

I am often asked why I have so much energy. Do I? I'm often told that I don't look my age. Don't I? I am happy to hear these comments, but I have always felt that there is nothing unusual about me. Until one day when I was vacationing in France.

I became friends with Angie, an English lady a little younger than I, who said, "You know, you are very inspiring. I admire your enthusiasm for life and your positive attitude. I wish some of it would rub off on me."

As I thought about her remark and I asked myself why I don't feel old or look my age, the answers became the inspiration and reason for writing this book.

I am an optimistic by nature and can always find a silver lining. In addition, my long love affair with fashion and beauty has taught me how important it is never to let go, and how much responsibility lies with each of us for our looks, self-confidence, and well being.

I don't know what attracted me to the world of fashion and made me decide to study dress design. Maybe growing up during the war wearing recycled clothes? I remember when my mother unraveled an old cardigan of my grandmother's and used the wool to knit a skirt for me (which I hated to wear. Worse yet, when it became too short, a piece of fabric was added, making it look hideous).

My involvement with the world of high fashion took many twists and turns. Each one was a new challenge and taught me new things.

While I was completing my studies in Paris, at Fleuri-Delaporte School of Design, the famous Swiss actress Liselotte Pulver asked me to create her dress for the occasion of meeting the Queen Mother, Princess Margaret, and her husband Lord Snowden at the Odeon Theater in London.

My first thought was *Oh, I am not ready for this—I won't be able to do it!*

I had been introduced to Liselotte by her sister Corinne Pulver, a friend of my mother. Corinne was working as a journalist in Paris, and she had taken an interest in my progress toward becoming a designer. Her confidence in me, and realizing what an honor this opportunity was, finally gave me the courage to go ahead.

My five years as a model—three years in Montreal, Canada, and two years in New York— taught me discipline that has never left me . . . and never will. To be hired by a photographer or art director for an assignment or ad campaign, one had to visit their studio on what was called a *go-see*.

Hair, makeup, and dress all had to be perfect, as if ready to step in front of the camera. (Today's models present themselves in jeans and a T-shirt, letting the pictures in their portfolio speak for them.)

But in those days, it was necessary to look good at all times, and until this day I follow that mantra. It has become second nature to me.

One day, while going down in the elevator with my daughter-in-law, Ann, and a lady who also lives in our building, the lady turned to me and said, "You always look so nice," and before I could say anything, Ann answered, "My mother-in-law looks nice, even when she is going to the laundry."

When my son Marc was only six months old, we did a shoot for a cover for the book *Nursing Your Baby* by Karen Pryor. The agency I worked through thought we had great potential to work as a mother-child team. But by then I was older, and as a mother, my priorities had changed. Therefore, I returned to my original training as a designer, and I opened a boutique in New York. I designed the clothes, and my mother took care of the clients.

During the years we had the store, I learned how insecure many women are about their style and what looks good on them. So five years later when our lease ran out, I became a fashion consultant. Besides working with individual clients, I gave workshops and wrote two books about fashion: *The Sensual Dresser* and *Dress to Impress*. (The latter was also translated into Chinese and published in China.)

Reinventing oneself is a phrase I often hear used, and doing so is certainly a way to stay active and feel alive. But when I first heard it, it puzzled me because all my life doing that came naturally to me.

A new challenge came when I was offered a job in a design studio; I worked there for a year before I was dismissed. Even though it happened a long time ago, I remember the day that happened like it was yesterday. Disappointed and angry—very angry—I left the studio, and I made myself a promise as I walked out: *I will never in my life work for anybody else again.* And I didn't.

Instead, I started my own design studio. It was not easy; I worked from home for the first year until I could rent a small space on Forty-Second Street in New York, just off Broadway. I sold painted or woven designs to apparel companies on Seventh Avenue, the fashion capital of the world, or to the home furnishing industry. My clients included Macy's, Spring Industries, Waverley, Donna Karan, Calvin Klein, Liz Claiborne, and many others. Part of the business was going to trade shows in Frankfurt and Brussels each year, and traveling to Paris and London to buy new merchandise to replenish our stock. I owned that business for many years.

I reinvented myself many times—I embraced new challenges, and I never lost my positive attitude or my willingness to try new things.

The hundreds of websites, social media posts, and

blogs about old age or getting older are proof that the millions of Americans over age fifty are concerned about or struggle with getting older. Some of the postings are serious, some are funny; some reassure us that getting older is not our fault or that it is not so bad. But there is always the underlying question, "How could this happen to me?"

"I used to be old, too, but it wasn't my cup of tea."

The answer is: *it happens to all of us.* But the attitude with which you accept this, and how you approach what lies ahead, will make the difference. All throughout life you were challenged and overcame difficulties; why should now be different? This is a new stage in your life, but not one you can't handle when you stay positive and engaged—and I hope this book will help you find the silver lining in your life, and you will feel like the lady on the left!

CHAPTER 1

It's Time to Get Over Growing Older

No, I won't tell you how old I am. If I do, you will see me with different eyes, and you will judge everything I do or say with that number in mind.

I made the mistake once of telling someone my age. I regretted it instantly and still do. Janet, a friend of mine living in Switzerland who is ten years younger than I, was visiting New York, and it was my birthday. We went to a bar to have a few drinks, when suddenly she said, "So, tell me, how old are you today?" And I fell into the trap.

Maybe it was the third glass of wine, or maybe it was because I knew I didn't look much older than she. Anyway, my ego took over, and I told her.

"Can I help you carry that?" she asked the next day when I was holding a small package. *Shit,* I thought, *why did I tell her?* Later, when she asked me if I would like to go to Costa Rica with her, she qualified that things are really quite comfortable there and I shouldn't worry.

Why would I worry? But she did, now that she knew my age.

It is often said that age is "only a number," and the

difference lies in what you do with that number. Sorry for the cliché, but this loosely translates into "You are only as old as you feel."

If Age Is Only a Number, Why Does Everyone Want to Know Mine?

Getting old is inevitable, but how soon you allow it to make decisions for you is your choice. I know that I am not ready for it, and I live my life without thinking about how old I am. Except when my birthday is coming up— that's always a reality check! Or when a friend says, "Isn't your birthday next week?"

"I don't have birthdays anymore," I say, "I stopped those years ago."

I often get a reaction like, "What a good idea!" Over the years, I have heard other people reply, "I am always thirty-nine" or "I have started to count backward."

As much as I would like to ignore my date of birth, the world will not. It is written on top of my driver's license . . . and it makes me slightly nervous when someone asks, "May I see some identification?" I always hope that he or she does not pay attention to my age, and luckily, they usually don't.

When I pick up my blood pressure medication, the pharmacist asks, "What is your date of birth?" I wonder if she couldn't see it in my file, or what knowing my age adds to my co-payment.

I answer in a low voice.

"Can you speak up, please?" she asks again.

I repeat it once more, and now everybody in the line

behind me knows how old I am. Most likely, nobody cares—but I do. You might call me vain, and maybe I am, but hearing myself say my age again and again reminds me of how old I am. It confirms it. This is something I can't allow, or it will settle in my brain and creep into in my bones, killing the spring in my step. Maybe it's a small spring, not like someone who is twenty-five or even forty, but I still walk erect, and I don't drag my feet.

Yes, age is only a number. But, oh, how it influences us if we are not careful. My friend Angela, who is very vibrant, active, and looks years younger than her age, recently had a birthday. When I asked her how she wanted to celebrate, she said, "Oh my God, this is a big one. I really don't feel like celebrating. Can you imagine? I will be X years old!"

(No, I won't tell on her.)

"It happens to all of us," I replied at the time, but she didn't hear me.

I noticed that after her birthday, Angela started every sentence with, "Well now, at my age," or "I don't know how long I can still do this," or "You never know, when one gets sick, seeing how old I am now . . ." She never had those thoughts before, but her last birthday gave her a terrible present—it robbed her of feeling *not old*.

"Please don't speak about your age all the time; it is starting to depress me," I said to her one day.

"But it is true, I am X years old now, and who knows what will happen, or if I will see my grandchildren graduate."

Getting a little impatient with her and not knowing what to say anymore, I quoted my grandmother, who all through my life was a beacon of wisdom for me: "You know, if you don't want to become old, you have to die young!"

Totally caught up in her new image of being old, she did not understand what I was trying to tell her, and continued to list all the things she would have trouble doing from now on.

I'm as Old (or Young) as I Need to Be

Hearing myself say my age out loud, and pointing out the negative aspects of it, will not only convince the world around me that I am old, but more important, it will make *me* feel old.

There was a time, long, long ago, when nobody dared to ask a lady her age. Even if somebody asked, she would never tell.

Today, people ask you all the time. I don't know why, or what difference it makes to them. Does the youth culture we live in really have such an influence? I am always surprised when someone asks my age, but I pull myself together and say, "Old enough!"

This is often followed by another question, usually something on the order of, "Now, really, how old are you? You can tell me! I won't tell anybody."

Fat chance!

If I were to tell her my age, I can hear her saying to her friends, "Can you imagine how old she is? She doesn't look her age. I thought she was younger, she looks younger!"

Another way to not reveal your age is to refuse to give a date to questions like "How long have you lived here already?"

My God, I have lived here forever and ever and ever, but will I tell you? NO!

"Oh, for a long time," I will say.

Another tricky question is "How old are your children?" We can't really lie about their ages, so I have to tell the truth. But who knows how old I was when I had my son? Maybe I was only eighteen. Or even younger!

Of course, not everybody tells the truth. When I was fourteen, my mother, Friedel, and I immigrated to Australia. On board the *Skaubryn*, a Norwegian passenger ship, Mother met Monsieur Fabre, the ship's purser. He was a suave, gray-haired Frenchman in his early fifties, who spoke with a soft voice and a charming accent. She asked me to say that I was twelve to make her look younger. I didn't understand. She was only thirty-six, and a good-looking, full-bosomed woman. Her blonde hair framed her pretty face, and her blue eyes twinkled mischievously when speaking to a man.

Maybe not wanting to be old runs in my family? The irony was that when we got to Australia and I tried to find a job because I didn't want to go to school anymore, I said I was eighteen. I got away with it because I looked quite mature—I mean, quite developed physically—and at that time, one didn't have to show any papers or proof of age. So after some training I became the paymaster in the Hotel Metropole in Sydney, Australia, for three years. The payroll covered more than 200 people, and I think if the manager, Mr. Langly, had known he was putting his employees' paychecks in the hands of a barely sixteen-year-old girl, he might have had second thoughts.

Refusing to think about, refer to, or mention your age—anytime, anywhere—will not make you forget about it entirely, but age will lose its importance. Not only will it change how you see yourself, but it will also change the way you look at others. If somebody is sixty-eight or seventy-three will not be important, but what matters is that they are young at heart.

You might have to practice a bit in the beginning and think before you speak. Avoid saying things like "When I was living in Paris in 1963 . . ." What a giveaway! Instead, just say, "When I was living in Paris . . ." This type of statement has two benefits: Besides not revealing your age, you're reminded of how lovely it was to live in Paris without focusing on how it was all a lifetime ago.

How Old Is Old?

It is interesting how, as we advance in years, we push the boundaries of what we consider "old age."

"I am so depressed," my friend Irma told me the other day.

When I asked why, she put her hands up in despair and answered, "I am turning thirty next week. I never thought I would get there."

No, none of us ever thinks that we will get "there." *What? Becoming thirty or forty or fifty? Or even older? No way! That happens to others—not me!* But as the years pile up, you'll find yourself kicking the idea of "old" farther and farther down the road.

When I was a child, I wondered why people like my grandparents looked so different. I can't remember my grandmother being anything but old. She wasn't old, she was only in her fifties, but fifty is an eternity from ten, and I *never* thought that one day I would be like her.

There's a line somewhere in the Bible that states, "Blessed are the ignorant." And I think the young are blissfully ignorant. Forgive me for using another cliché (I think clichés hang around so long because they tell the truth), but "youth is wasted on the young." For a long time, I did not understand the meaning of it, probably because I was one of those ignorant young people. When I wasn't young anymore, it clicked. Youth is wasted on them because they take their good fortune for granted, not realizing that it won't last. To quote my grandmother again, "The only good thing about aging is that it happens to everybody."

Irma was right: the first hurdle is thirty. At that age, you are no longer a girl, but a young woman. And just when you grow used to it, you turn forty. Now that is a real game changer. You are then a woman, and here and there, little wrinkles show up. What saves you in your forties is that for most women, life is so busy with careers, children, or both, that you don't have too much time to analyze the whys and hows of your changing body and attitudes.

During your fifties, you begin to realize that your body is irrevocably changing. Typically, women experience menopause—and hot flashes, of course. But speaking for myself, I was never happier than when "that part of me" was out of the way. *What a relief! No more cramps, no more mood swings, no more fear of pregnancy—just the joy of sex!*

And Then You're Sixty

Sixty is now called the new forty. Wonderful! Somebody turned back the clock. You don't have to think of yourself as old yet, even though seventy is looming on the horizon. But when seventy approaches, you know this is a huge threshold. Unfortunately, nobody calls it the new fifty—it is seventy, plain and simple. And I have seen many of my friends struggle with the idea of being seventy. They don't want parties, they don't want cards, and they just want to forget about it.

I remember when my mother turned seventy. We were vacationing in Marbella, Spain, and we were happy to celebrate her birthday during the holidays, especially since every one she loved was there.

I got up early to prepare a special breakfast for her, but when I came out of the bedroom at 7:30 a.m., she was already sitting on the terrace drinking a cup of coffee.

"You are up early. It is your birthday—you deserve to sleep longer!"

When I put my arm around her shoulders to kiss her, I saw that she was crying.

"Why are you crying?"

"Because it is my birthday."

"But that is no reason to cry," I said.

"Yes, it is a reason this year!"

"What is different this year?" I asked out of ignorance.

"You really don't understand, do you? I am seventy today!"

No, I didn't understand. How could I? I was still so far away from being seventy.

"Please don't cry. We will make this a happy day," I told her.

"It cannot be happy. I am seventy now," she repeated, covering her eyes with her handkerchief.

Her mood didn't change all day, and even the candlelight dinner we had organized for her on the beach did not cheer her up. I went to bed that night puzzled and wondering if I would feel that way when my turn came.

Reaching your eighties is a different story, a much better story. You are proud of how old you are and happy to have made it so far.

When a woman asks me to guess her age, I know she must be over eighty, and before answering, I subtract five years from how old I think she is.

"Let's see. Maybe seventy-eight, or at most eighty?"

"Oh, no! I am eighty-six!" she'll say, with an air of pride and satisfaction.

"Really? I didn't think so."

"Yes, I know most people don't think I am as old as I am," she'll say, with another big smile. "God willing, I will have another few years to go."

Maybe I should be truthful, but I think the happy reaction is worth a little white lie.

Yes, there are those days when you are rewarded for your wrinkles by still being alive.

I recall watching actor Rob Lowe during an interview with Oprah Winfrey. They were talking about age, and he said, "Put it this way: when we get older, there is a fork in the road, and we have the choice to take the right turn and let go, or take the left turn and fight to stay young."

The choice is yours: will you turn right or left? I know I am turning left!

CHAPTER 2

Getting Carded

"May I see your ID?" is a normal question when a twenty-two-year-old goes to a club, but when I buy a bottle of wine and the man at the register asks me for my identification, I always ask, "Really?" He nods, and I hand over my driver's license. I am told it is the law to see the ID of people who buy alcohol. Probably so, but I am left wondering what happened to common sense?

My son told me that there are places like bars and discotheques that ask for ID to make their female patrons feel better. A nice idea when one is forty or fifty, but past that? If I don't remember that it is the law, I feel like somebody is kidding me.

Not Ready Yet

For many years, I received letters from the AARP telling me about the benefits of becoming a member. Each time I saw an envelope with their logo, I wouldn't even open it. Instead, I dropped it straight into the wastepaper basket, thinking, *Not yet!*

But time marched on, and during a visit to Buckingham Palace in London, I was very surprised by a young man who was about twenty years old and sitting behind the glass window at the ticket office. Without asking me about myself, he simply said, "One senior?"

I looked behind me. Was he speaking to me? Yes, he was! *Are people in England becoming seniors before we do in the United States?* I wondered.

I didn't find out, but after having the hefty fee of forty British pounds reduced by half, I walked away, thinking: *Well, if I have to be a senior citizen, what better place to start old age than at Buckingham Palace?*

As I was sitting in a lawyer's office for a real estate closing, the lawyer suddenly turned to me and asked, "You are a senior, right?"

"What? Oh, yes, I am."

Noticing my hesitation, the young, very attractive real estate agent tried to help me out: "But you wear it so well!"

Some years later, I met that same real estate agent again. We exchanged the usual pleasantries before he said, "I must tell you something: you certainly did a good job taking care of yourself!"

Was that a compliment, or did he want to sell me another house?

"One way ticket to Summit, senior citizen, please. Do you want to see my card?"

"Not necessary."

The short and sure answer came from the girl behind the window. I felt disappointed. Was my status as a senior so evident, or was she just lazy?

On another day, one of her colleagues was kinder.

"One way ticket to Summit, senior citizen, please."

Before handing me my ticket, she leaned closer to her microphone and said, "You look really good for a senior citizen!"

I am not the only one who gets a shock when the world doesn't see us as young anymore. I remember when Pierre, my significant other, came to the office one morning looking displeased.

"What is the matter?" I asked him.

"Can you imagine a young girl offered me a seat? Do I look so old?"

"No, you don't," I reassured him. "It's your white hair." Although he still had a lot of hair, it *was* all white.

"Really? You think so?" he asked, relieved.

I met Pierre when his hair was still black, when he was only forty-three. He had picked me up in the Hotel Dorchester in London, a truth he always changed when telling somebody how we met.

"We were introduced at a party," he would explain. He thought it sounded more dignified than a casual encounter in a hotel. I had gone to meet an old friend, and when I found out that my friend had not shown up, I was disappointed and angry. When I took the elevator down, it stopped on the ninth floor, and Pierre stepped in. "Good afternoon. How are you?"

I didn't even answer.

Just before we reached the ground floor, he asked if I would like to have tea with him.

Not knowing what to do next, and not being in a very good mood, I replied, "Why not?"

Tea is served in the lobby of the Hotel Dorchester, which faces the revolving door. While sitting there, I hoped I would see my lost date arrive. He didn't, and so I spent the rest of the afternoon listening to Pierre tell me that he was separated from his wife, that he was chairman of a Swiss multinational company in the United States and lived in Chicago, but that he often went to New York to meet with their advertising agency. At the end of the afternoon, he asked if he could call me during one of his visits to New York.

"Why not?" I said again.

A few weeks later (I had forgotten about him by then), he called and invited me to the theater. We saw *Mama Mia* and went to Regine's (a discotheque on Park Avenue in New York at the time) for dinner—and that was the start of a long, happy relationship without being married . . . or maybe because of it?

But Pierre was not the only one who got reality checks. The same thing happened to my friend Karen, a pretty brunette whose face does not say sixty-six.

"Can you imagine a young man offered me a seat? Really! It made me feel so old."

"Do you remember there was a time when being polite had nothing to do with age, but with gender?" I reminded her. "Thank goodness some men still feel that way and you met one."

"You are right," she said, laughing while picking up her glass of wine. "I may have overreacted."

These little reminders come in many different ways. One day when my friend Jackie was shopping, the cashier offered her a discount for seniors without asking. She accepted the discount, but was unhappy to be labeled a "senior" without her permission.

Wrapping Your Head Around the "S" Word

It took me a long time to get used to the word *senior*. Once I was eligible for a reduced fare Metro card for senior citizens, I took several weeks to request the application and another ten days to fill it out. How vain can one be?

I finally completed the form on a rainy Sunday afternoon, and on the way to work the next day, I had the required photo taken—but I only remembered to do it after I was halfway to the subway station. Had I passed the photo place on purpose? Who knows how the subconscious works?

Before I could submit the application, I had to have it notarized. The notary looked over the form, and then at me. Satisfied the two matched, she signed it.

I felt depressed as I left the bank, and I tried to shake the feeling by reminding myself that I was going to save three dollars a day. But it did not work. After all, what good is a few dollars when one's ego is at stake?

After a few weeks, an official-looking letter arrived, you know, the one with a big window and bold letters printed on it: "IMPORTANT—OPEN IMMEDIATELY." I wondered what it could be. Out came a card, just like a credit card, with my picture, my name, and SENIOR CITIZEN printed on it in big letters and followed by a huge R, which stood for *reduced*. *Reduced to what?* was my first thought. I took it personally, but I found out that referred to the fare.

When the time came to put money on the card, I greeted the bearded, friendly man from whom I had bought my Metro cards for years with an upbeat "Hi!" that was more cheerful than I felt. I handed him the card and the money and waited.

"What? *You?*" he asked, looking at the card.

I nodded with a brave smile.

"Well, I wouldn't have thought so."

He couldn't have said anything nicer, but then again, I always knew he was a kind man.

When trying to use the card for the first time, I made quite sure that while passing it at the turnstile my hand covered the REDUCED FARE part with my picture.

"Turn the card around," came a loud voice from the booth, "or it won't work."

So much for privacy.

But since then, I have found a way to avoid traveling as a senior when I don't want to be seen as a SENIOR. I have purchased a regular Metro card and when I don't want the person I am traveling with to know that I am a senior, I take out my yellow and blue card, swipe it, and nobody calls out, "Turn the card around!"

Why should they? I am just like everybody else—right?

Oh, by the way, I have an AARP card now!

CHAPTER 3

Is Your Glass Half Full or Half Empty?

One morning I went to pick up my passport. The clerk asked me to check if the information was correct, and when I came to the expiration date, I saw the new passport was good for ten years. Wow!! Ten years. That's a long time. For one short moment, I wondered if that might be my last passport . . . but pushing the imaginary delete button I have installed in my mind to get rid of negative thoughts, I decided to share the Embassy's optimism. If they think I need a passport for that long, who am I to question it? Looking at the positive side was a real ego booster.

Push the Delete Button

Do you have a delete button in your mind for negative thoughts?

It is just as useful in your mind as it is on your computer. Whenever you push it, it clears away what you don't want anymore. It gets rid of unpleasant thoughts that have crept up. It is just a little trick to help you keep your optimism alive.

Although optimism is a plus at any stage in life, it is especially important when we get older. Doctors and psychiatrists have confirmed that it will guarantee you a longer, happier live.

We know that the road ahead is shorter than the one behind us. Therefore, staying optimistic will make this road smoother, helping us avoid the potholes and cobblestones we might otherwise stumble over.

The Most Important Word in Your Vocabulary

We do not lose enthusiasm because we are getting older. We begin to age through loss of enthusiasm. One can be a victim of age or its master. Psychiatrist Eric Berne, author of *Games People Play,* put it this way: "A healthy person goes, 'Yes,' 'No,' and 'Whoopee!' An unhealthy person goes, 'Yes but,' 'No but,' and 'No whoopee.'"[1]

Because the word whoopee, or *wow* as we say today, is the most important of the three, you must never lose your curiosity, your ability to be surprised, your wish to learn, your desire to be a part of what goes on around you, and your capacity to recognize when something deserves a *wow!*

Recognizing that something is *wow!* will stop you from feeling old. It will stop you from thinking that something is not for you anymore—because it is. Staying in touch with current events through television, newspapers, theater,

---

1. Eric Berne. AZQuotes.com, Wind and Fly LTD, 2016. www.azquotes .com/author/1308-Eric_Berne, accessed January 12, 2016.

lectures, and movies (just to name a few) keeps you aware of the world you live in.

Stay Current to Stay Young

Unfortunately, nobody comes knocking at your door, pulling you out of your comfortable recliner or sofa to take you to the movies. But movies are an exciting, easy way to stay in touch. I say easy because it is an activity easily done alone.

"*Uh-oh! They seem to have loved it!*"

"What, you go alone to the movies?" some of my friends ask.

"Yes, why not? We don't talk anyway, do we?"

It might help that I am a movie buff, but having said that, I also go to the movies to see what is going on in the world. Movies reflect the time we live in; they always have. Often a movie is not my taste, but I feel that I must find out why it is so popular that it takes in over $100,000 in ticket sales during the first weekend.

Even if I don't like the movie, once I've seen it, at least I know where the world is coming from.

Movies for kids were never part of my program until my grandchildren, Remy and Cosette, were born. Once they were old enough, taking them to the movies became our thing. I was happy to spend time with them, even if I wasn't looking forward to *Bob the Builder*. But that soon changed.

The children happily settled in their seats, and eating pretzels was a good beginning. When the trailers for upcoming events played, they would point their little thumbs up or down, and whichever movie had the most thumbs up was the one we would see next.

No, *Penguins of Madagascar* is not *The King's Speech*, but after seeing *Frozen*, I thanked the kids for taking me. I say *taking me* because I never in a hundred years would have gone to see it. I saw it three times and bought a copy. Just goes to show, you never know where the *wow* comes from, and unless you are out there, you might miss it.

My visit to a little town in upstate New York, where I followed my passion of going to garage sales, was one of those *wow* moments.

As we looked over the treasures, a young, bearded, heavy-set lad, about thirty years old, turned to me and said, "Nice day today, isn't it?"

"We are lucky that it doesn't rain like it did yesterday," I agreed.

We both moved on. A few minutes later, he stood next to me again and said in a low voice, "You know, you still got it."

"Got what?" was my first reaction, but then I understood that his remark was meant as a compliment.

"Thank you," I responded. "You made my day."

Noticing my surprise, he winked. While walking away, he repeated reassuringly, "You really do!"

Wow.

My Happiness Collection

The reason I am always happy to get a compliment is not just my vanity—although there is some of that, too—but the real reason is that I can add them to my happiness collection, which I started long ago.

One year, my friend Wendy and I were having a few drinks to celebrate another birthday. While sitting at a bar among our peers and the young after-work crowd, I said, "I wonder if my bag of compliments will help me through the darker days ahead."

"What are you talking about?" she asked.

"It is a little game that I have been playing with myself most of my life. Do you want to hear about it?"

"Sure!" Wendy laughed. "It must be another one of your funny ideas."

"It started when I was very young. Every time somebody said something nice about my looks, or about what I had done, I put the words carefully in my memory bag, which I carry in my heart. I believe that a compliment is a gift one should be grateful for and cherish. One day when the compliments stop, I will have something to fall back on."

"How is that?" Wendy asked, trying not to laugh.

"Well, when the days of wine and roses are over and no one pays any attention to me anymore, I will open my bag and cheer myself up with the proof of the wonderful life I have had."

"Are you sure your bag is full enough now to last until the end of your life?" Wendy asked, starting her third glass of wine.

"No, there is still plenty of room. That is why I am not ready to be old yet!"

Clinking her glass against mine she said, "Why don't we drink to that? Cheers!"

Looking Forward

One year our family leased a house for summer vacation in the South of France, and on the ground floor was another apartment for rent. One day, Monsieur Girard, our landlord, told us he had rented it to a very nice

Belgian lady who would move in the following week.

Once she had settled in, I went to welcome her. Monsieur Girard had not mentioned how old she was. All he told us was that she was a single woman. Therefore, I was a little surprised when I saw her, and even more so when she told me that she was eighty-five and had just signed a five-year lease.

"I want to spend my summers here. I hate the cold and just love France."

I wanted to tell her how I admired her for being so positive—but how could I? How could I put a doubt in her mind that she might not spend the next five summers in the sunshine of France? When I left her an hour and a half later, all I could think was, *Maybe I, too, can be somebody's neighbor in the South of France when I am eighty-five years old!*

But even if I won't become eighty-five, being positive fills all the days I have left with more joy, more life, and more hope to do all the things I still want to do.

What would life be without hope?

CHAPTER 4

Sex Has No Age

Helen Gurley Brown was the editor of *Cosmopolitan* magazine for thirty-two years. She used the pages of the magazine to help women find themselves and become who they wanted to be. But she never forgot to emphasize how important sex is to our happiness. In her own words, "Sex is wonderful. If you are not having sex, what a shame! And beside eating and breathing, it's one of the three best things in life."

Even in her later years, she never changed her mind about sex. When she was ninety, she still felt that it should always be a part of your life. I have never agreed with anything more, and sharing my experiences and my challenges in finding sex might inspire you not to look the other way when somebody is looking at you. No, it's not too late, and it never will be. Love and sex can blossom even late in life.

When Pierre died, I had only one wish—besides wanting him back. I prayed, "Dear God, please let me fall in love one more time before I die." He heard me, and I will never stop thanking him for making me feel whole again. But it did not happen immediately.

I struggled for the next two years before I even

considered meeting somebody. I had a difficult time being alone. Suddenly there were no more phone calls, no more flowers, no more jokes, and no more love—just loneliness. I floated in a vacuum.

When I started looking around, I didn't like or want what I saw. All I saw were old men. Yes, Pierre was an old man too when he died, but he was *my* old man. We had spent many years growing old together. He was like an old shoe I had worn for a long time, one that fit well and was comfortable.

When the time came to move on, I didn't know how. Some of my friends suggested Match.com, an Internet dating service, so I tried it. After answering half of the questions, doubt made me stop. Who would want me? All the profiles I read were of perfect, nonsmoking, nondrinking, walking-in-the-sunset, classical-music-loving men looking for their perfect match. I belonged to the "across a crowded room" generation, and this was not for me.

Then my friend Tamie suggested I look at the personal ads in the Sunday *New York Times* (which had PERSONALS then). I didn't get the *Times* on Sunday, but my neighbor did. So early on Sunday morning, I sneaked out and took the page with the ads. No, he didn't need it. He was a good-looking young man of about thirty with a girlfriend (I had seen her leaving his apartment some mornings).

Reading the ads, I wondered again why these perfect, physically fit men with warm personalities, a love for music, and experience in traveling all around the world had to advertise. I read those ads for at least ten weeks before I got up enough nerve to make the call. I decided to call two of them.

The charge was \$2.99 for the connection and \$2.99 for each minute after that. A long menu telling me to press this or that button also counted, and my bill was \$47.00 for those two calls. Once I had pressed the right buttons, the voice of the man who had placed the ad asked me to leave my name and number, and he promised to call back. But nobody called back.

So I kept reading more ads, and I tried my luck again. This time two men called back.

The first one sounded very nice, and I was pleased to hear from him.

"How tall are you?" he asked, toward the end of the conversation.

Oh, he must be short, I thought.

"Five-nine," I answered.

Silence.

"I am five-four, would that be a problem?" he asked.

I took a deep breath. "Yes, I think so."

I was glad for his honesty, and for not wasting each other's time.

The next caller was a freelance photographer, divorced, no children, who spent most weekends taking photos. He asked, "Where would you like to meet?"

I picked a bar close to my office.

"Oh, I don't drink! What about Starbucks on Friday at four p.m.?"

I agreed, and his parting words were, "I wear glasses, have gray hair, a gray beard, and will be wearing a gray shirt."

He hung up before I could say that I didn't like the color gray.

Sitting in Starbucks on a bench near the window on Friday at 4:00 p.m., I looked at the black coffee he'd ordered for me. No, he had not asked what type of coffee I liked, and while he was telling me that he spent all his weekends taking photos and wouldn't mind to have a companion help him carry his bags, I was thinking of an excuse to leave.

"I am sorry, but I have to catch a train to New Jersey at four forty-five," I finally said. He seemed glad that I had to take a train, and I was glad to get away.

After that I took some time off, until a colleague arranged a blind date for me with a German fellow called Heinz.

"Shall we meet at TGIF on Friday, say at noon?" he asked. "Do you know where it is?"

"I think so," I said.

"Well, don't worry if you don't," he said. "One can't know everything." Then he gave me directions for how to get there.

"You are German, right?" he asked.

My accent must have given me away. "Yes."

"So am I."

I was encouraged and felt that being from the same corner of the world might be a plus. "Well, I will see you on Wednesday!"

"It might be a good idea to confirm on Tuesday," he answered.

"Very well, until Tuesday then."

Tuesday came and had nearly gone when he called around eight o'clock that night.

"I was just looking at the weather, and it looks like we will have snow or freezing rain tomorrow. If that is so, we might want to postpone."

Good start: if a little snow or rain will prevent us from meeting, how keen can a guy be? But I agreed and suggested that we check the next morning around 10 to see what the weather was like.

At 10:00 a.m., the phone rang.

"Well, we are lucky again," he said.

When were we lucky before? I wondered and then answered, "Yes, we are. So I will see you at noon."

"I will be wearing a black leather jacket and be sitting at the bar, so you will recognize me."

"Okay, I am tall and blond."

"That might not help me."

"Why not?" I asked.

"You might be wearing a hat, then how can I see that your hair is blond?"

"I never wear hats."

"Oh!"

At that point, I said, "See you later." I hung up, wondering if this might be a bad idea, but then again, if you don't try . . .

By the time I left the house, it was raining like someone was emptying buckets of water onto the road, but I bravely drove through the torrent. While driving, I tried to imagine what Heinz might look like: *leather jacket . . . mmhmm . . . maybe he is a sporty, relaxed guy . . . not stuffy.* Then, a strange image flashed through my mind, which made me laugh aloud. I saw a man who had a front tooth missing.

I arrived, twenty-five minutes too early, at the shopping center where TGIF was located. I am always early even if I try to be late. But that day I did not want to be the first one. So I stayed in the car and read a newspaper until noon. The rain had not stopped. At five past twelve, with my umbrella protecting me, I walked into the restaurant.

There indeed was a man in a black leather jacket sitting at the bar facing the main door.

When he saw me, he got off of the stool.

"Hello, you must be Brigitte?" He greeted me with a big smile that exposed a toothless gap in the front of his mouth!

"Hi," I stammered, remembering my vision while driving.

"Now I can take off my jacket," he said happily. With that comment, he exposed a wrinkled khaki shirt that had seen better days.

"What would you like to drink?"

"White wine, please," I answered.

While I sipped my drink, he talked about himself, first in German and then in English.

"Now, I am single. But I had a very ugly divorce. I don't even want to go there."

Neither did I. As I continued listening to him, I wondered what I was doing there with this strange man. His hair was short, curly, pepper-and-salt, and unruly. He wore rimless glasses, and his skin must have taken many years to become as shriveled and dry as it was.

Suddenly, I couldn't erase Pierre's image from my mind. Except for going to the beach, he never went without a coat and tie. He took special care of his graying, slightly curly hair, and except for early mornings, I never saw him unshaven. He wore his well-tailored clothes with ease and confidence—the same ease and confidence with which he did everything in his life, never forgetting that living well was a priority.

Heinz's voice brought me back to reality. "I will just take an appetizer," he said.

I took this to be my cue not to get carried away with anything over $9.95.

My salad arrived.

"The portions are certainly big," I commented, looking at my plate.

"You can always take it home for tomorrow," he said. "It can make another meal."

I did not reply. I just pondered how delicious a salad could really be the next day.

"Do you dance well?" he suddenly asked.

The question and vision of us on the dance floor together sent shock waves through me. "No, I don't."

"How come?"

"My mother didn't think dance lessons were necessary. She believed that one can either dance or not. Rhythm is something one is born with, she would say, so I never became a good dancer."

After a moment of silence he said, "Well, it doesn't matter—I can lead."

My heart sank, and all I could think was, *Please don't lead, not on the dance floor or anywhere else.*

By now about an hour and a half had passed, and after asking if I wanted another drink, which I declined because I was driving, Heinz asked for the check. When the waitress placed it on the table, I took my purse out and hesitantly asked, "How much is my part?"

He studied the yellow slip and then said, "Including the tip, fifteen dollars."

The waitress came and took the money.

"I would like to see you again, to practice my German." He hurried to correct his faux pas. "Of course, you know that is not the reason . . . I really like you."

After enjoying Pierre's generosity for so many years, I could not believe that this man—who said he wanted to see me again—would not spare $15.00.

"Let me walk you to your car."

I smiled at him, and we shook hands before I drove away. When I got home, there was an email from him asking me if he could contact me soon with suggestions on how we could spend more time together.

Trying to let him down easy, I told him that it was too soon and that I was not ready to spend time with anybody yet.

My next experience was much better, but didn't offer a solution either. Brian and I met at a trade show I attended in New York. We exchanged business cards before parting. A few days later he called and asked if I wanted to have a drink with him. I hesitated, he was twenty-two years younger than I, but his "bad boy" image attracted me, and I thought of it as an exciting new adventure. We had agreed to meet at a restaurant in New Jersey, where he lived. He was already there when I arrived.

"How would you like a cocktail?" I loved the way he

said cocktail instead of drink, and while we were having our cocktails all his attention was on me.

"How about eating something?" he asked after the second drink.

The waitress seated us at a table for two, right at the window. The fading light of the day made the flowers, which grew close to the window, look like happy little faces smiling at me, much like Brian's eyes. He wanted to know about my life, and he told me about his.

"I love the way you dress," he said, "and what is that around your neck?"

The story behind the little golden bear charm swinging on its chain prompted him to tell me all about his hunting adventures.

Although he had a "bad boy" vibe, he was an ordinary-looking fellow, just about my height, with a receding hairline, a swag in his step, and awkward manners. None of that mattered, because for the first time in years I felt alive. I was happy.

When a few hours later the parking attendant brought my car, Brian kissed me on the cheek, and holding my hand, he said, "Would you like to have a night cap? I don't live far from here."

Another two years passed before God answered my prayer.

Seeing the World Through Rose-Colored Glasses

After swallowing another piece of kebab, Hassan suddenly asked me, "Do you know that sex has no age?"

Embarrassed, I looked down at my plate. Did he really

just say that? I hadn't heard anything better in years. It was music to my ears, especially since I was attracted to him.

We were traveling together for two weeks. He was a take-charge person, and I liked nothing better. I was on cloud nine. Halfway through our journey, it happened.

The reason I have always fallen in love with men of authority, men who take charge, can be traced to my childhood. It goes back to World War II when I was growing up without my father. He was never present in my life. To this day, when I hear somebody say "my father," I feel the void, and when I think back about the choices I made in picking men, they were always influenced by my desire— my need—to find a father.

Being on cloud nine lasted longer than I had hoped for. While our attraction for each other grew, the opportunity to be together did not. We were living in separate worlds, and in countries far apart.

Maybe I should have had the wisdom to know when it was time to let go. But I didn't, and today I am glad I didn't, because now, five years later, we are still in touch. Every year, we manage to steal a few happy moments from life, and those happy moments carry us forward to the next year.

There have been many happy moments, like the day we went to the Red Sea and ate fish with our hands.

"Do you mind eating with your fingers?" Hassan asked while he was digging into his first victim.

I caught myself quickly. "No, no . . . not at all," I lied. With that, I took the first fish apart, but at the end of the meal I really enjoyed my "finger-licking" way of eating fish. It made me feel local, and closer to Hassan.

His warm, penetrating brown eyes and his unshakeable self-confidence made up for his short stature and for not having much hair anymore.

One time, when he came to pick me up from the airport in Cairo, and I complimented him on the polka-dot print shirt he wore, he told me: "You have no idea how many times I changed my shirt before coming to pick you up. I felt like a teenager going to his first dance."

Teenager. Dancing. How wonderful! I thought, and it made me giggle like a teenager too.

Another time, we sang along with the radio while driving on the New York State Thruway to go shopping at the Woodbury Commons. Or there was the time when I was sitting in the lobby of my hotel and anxiously watching the door, and my heart beat a little faster to see him arrive.

Yes, these are all simple events, I know, but when you wear rose-colored glasses, everything is *pink*.

While driving back to Cairo one evening in total darkness (there are no streetlights on the country roads in Egypt), Hassan held my hand and said, "Love always hurts."

When I didn't answer, he went on.

"Did you ever notice that most love songs are sad? Why do you think this is?"

I didn't know. I didn't want to know, because at that moment my world was perfect.

"And this one is my grandma and her current lover."

My Gift Box

Maybe love hurts because the highlights it gives your life are just that—highlights—like the sun flooding your world in a golden glow some days only to disappear at night.

Oh, I know there might be a day when Hassan won't be wearing the polka-dot shirt anymore, and I won't arrive at the airport anymore—and that will be the day I put my precious memories in the gift box I have waiting. I call it a gift box because the affection and love I found so late in life will always be a special gift—and the ribbon I will tie around the box won't allow the memories to fade . . . that said, maybe I won't need the box for a long while to come.

Could there be a gift box waiting for you somewhere too?

As you can see, there might be a few detours, some ups and downs before you meet somebody. Or I can hear you say, *I am not looking for anybody, I am fine alone,* and I am sure you are, but sharing, touching, and being two is better than eating alone!

I recently saw an interview on television where six seniors living in Florida in a retirement home were asked about their sex lives. Yes, they each had one. An eighty-six-year-old man told the interviewer that his sex life had never been better.

A woman in her seventies said, "I have never enjoyed sex as much as now."

It has become common knowledge that there is a lot going on in retirement communities. In the AARP Bulletin of June 2015, an article by Paula Spencer Scott titled *Sex in the Nursing Home* explains how important sex is for their residents, and how facilities are coping with the new challenge.

Good for them, they are not as retired as the world thinks!

My mother lived the last eighteen months of her life in the Sunrise Assisted Living facility in Basking Ridge. While we were having lunch together one day in the dining room of the home, she suddenly pointed to a couple sitting a few tables away from us and said, "Look at those two over there. I know they are playing footsy under the table, and I wonder what else they do."

She did not sound happy saying it; maybe she was a

little envious? And during another visit, when I saw the man she had pointed out go into the lady's room, I did not tell her about it.

My friend Alice O'Conner, who just turned 100, was born in Switzerland. After arriving in the United States, she worked as a private nurse at the Roosevelt Hospital in New York. When the Shah of Iran, Mohammad Reza Pahlavi, was in New York for treatment, he was her patient. With great pride she showed me the letter he had sent her thanking her for her care and kindness.

When she retired she started painting, writing poetry, and working part time at The Unity Center, where she met Ann Theresa and Justin. Today she lives in a nursing home in New York. Since all her relatives live in Switzerland, Ann Theresa, her boyfriend Justin, and I have become her family. When we visit her, I am sad to say, she often does not recognize Ann Theresa and me. But when she sees Justin, her face always lights up, and she says with a big smile, "Ohhhhhh, it's you!"

At that moment, Ann Theresa and I become invisible.

What a relief it is to know that *that part* of us doesn't die until we do.

How reassuring it is to know that your age doesn't matter, and neither does the age of your partner. Therefore, don't slam the door shut when an opportunity comes knocking. Remember instead that sex has no age!

CHAPTER 5

The Persistence of Memory

Memories are persistent, and they are like phantoms that follow you. Some make you cry, some make you laugh, and others bring back the joy of happy moments. They crack open doors you might have closed long ago, allowing you to walk backward in time to relive a happy moment or event, or bring you back to places where you were happy.

A few weeks ago, I suddenly felt like visiting my father's grave. But I couldn't do so because he is buried in Germany in a little town called Kronach. I spent my summer vacations as a child there, visiting my Aunt Lisl and Uncle Fritz. They owned a beauty salon for men and women. Instead of playing in the garden, I passed my days in the salon watching Uncle Fritz spray perfume on the ladies after they had had their hair done, and complimenting them on their look.

He was a short and heavyset man with a big belly and no hair. But when he looked over his thick glasses, with a twinkle in his blue eyes and flashing his disarming smile, I found him very handsome. Sometimes when my Aunt

Lisl thought he was exaggerating with his praise for his customers, she said, "Fritz, stop it. If you put it on too thick, they won't believe you."

The salon was divided into two sections, one for women and one for men, separated by a wall with a door connecting them. Because there were fewer male customers than female, Klaus was the only barber. I liked to watch him cut the men's hair. And I noticed that often before a client went to pay, Klaus would open a drawer next to where he kept the scissors and combs and hand a small envelope to the man. When I asked what it was, Klaus dismissed me with a short, "It's not for little girls."

That was the wrong answer. It made me determined to find out what it was. So one day when there were no clients and Klaus had gone to lunch, I went to the drawer and looked at the little envelopes, and to my surprise, one of them was open. I saw no harm in looking inside—but I did more. I took the white rubber tube out of the envelope.

Wondering what it was, I pulled it over my fingers, and stretching it a little nearly covered all of them. Forgetting that it was "not for little girls," I rushed to my uncle.

"Uncle Fritz, what is this for?" I asked.

He didn't tell, but instead sternly ordered me to put it back immediately and never open that drawer again.

I did as I was told, and it was not until I was a "big girl" that I found out what it was for.

On that particular day, a memory of my father resurrected my aunt and uncle for me, and it brought me back to a place where I was happy.

You need your memories to know who you are and where you came from. No, not all memories are happy ones, but if you find a way of letting go of the pain, even those memories can teach you something. They can make your future look brighter by showing you how important every moment in your life is *now*.

Just before my mother died, she wrote me this letter (her English never became perfect, but I always knew what she meant):

Christmas 2004

Dear Brigitte,

My dear little Muchilein,

Again it is Christmas and we are still together. For how much longer?

At this time of the year I often think of our dear ones who have left already so long ago—Vati, Oma, Guenther and many others. It is a nostalgic trip into the past.

I think of the Christmases where one could not buy anything, and yet tried to make the celebration of light one of hope. Because nearly every one of us had a family member on the front lines, and the worry about them was always with us. Ach, how little material things did we need then?

I tried very hard and did as well as I could to be father and mother to you, while being a young, inexperienced young woman. But with you on my side we made the best of it, and being my little companion, already at a young age, you stood bravely by me. We can truly say that we went through thin and thick together.

Now you are grown up and a lot has changed—time, things and people. But for me these memories are like precious stones which light up the way that lies behind me.

Memory is a paradise from which one can't be expelled. I, for my part am nearly on the end of my long journey and I know I don't need to worry about you. You will always find the right way without me, but my love stays behind and will always follow you.

So for today we will stop digging around in the past, instead look forward with hope to the future.

I thank you, my dear daughter for your tender care and love that you have shown me all your life. May God protect you and give you a long healthy life. This I wish for you with all my heart.

Loving you always,
Mutti

Yes, my mother's letter brought forth tears, and with them came the memory of our life together—wonderful moments and painful events.

World War II changed my mother from a young and innocent girl into an independent, self-assured woman who became, for many years, both mother and father to me. This was a change my father, Bruno, had difficulty dealing with when he returned home from being a soldier for six years and a prisoner of war in France for four years. His death shortly after returning home made my mother decide to move to Australia, where she hoped we could start a new life.

Without speaking the language, without money, and without any friends or family close by, our start was difficult. However, with my mother's resolve and determination, we eventually settled in.

The day she met Caesar, an Armenian accountant, her guardian angel must have been around. Caesar was a heavy-set little man, about whom she would sometimes say, "Look at him: he has short legs, a belly, and no hair. How can I have fallen so in love with him?"

She was hopelessly in love, and they were inseparable. I was happy for her, and understood that love had not as much to do with her attraction to Caesar as his fulfilling a part of her that had been starved for the ten years my father was away.

When Jacques, my future husband, walked into the deli my mother was managing, it was *my* happy moment. He had arrived from Paris only a few weeks before, and in contrast to the Australian boys, he appeared to come from a different planet. He was dressed in the latest French fashion, and he spoke with a charming accent in broken English. I remember the day as if it was yesterday. My mother had called me to come into the store (we lived on the first floor), to help her serve the customers. When I walked in, Jacques was the only one there. Despite that I was wearing my oldest pair of pants and a horribly worn-out sweater, Jacques came every night to shop. He became our best customer, my boyfriend, and, two years later, my husband.

Those were carefree and happy times that nobody can take away from me!

Unfortunately, too often in life we don't appreciate or recognize what we have, or had. But at this point in life, allowing your experience to guide you will make you more appreciative and allow you to do things differently. It will prevent repeating mistakes you have made in the past, like concentrating too much on your work instead of spending more time with your spouse or family.

When Jane, my longtime friend, asked her father on his deathbed if he had any regrets, he answered in a feeble voice, "Yes, I wish I would have taken more taxis."

I do take more taxis now, but the big change I have made is to buy fewer *things*. I don't need more *things*, I need to make more memories for me, for my friends, and for my family, who don't need more *things* either.

Presents are appreciated the moment you give them, but are often forgotten soon after. When I ask my grandson a few months after Christmas, "Do you remember what you got for Christmas, Remy?" he looks at me, surprised, like *Should I?* When he sees I am still waiting for an answer he says, "Not really. I remember some Legos, but I don't know who gave them to me."

No memory here, no trace of a special moment. But a present such as an invitation to a special restaurant, or buying tickets to the theater or a show your family would otherwise not see, or taking a trip as a family or with a friend, are moments you and your family will never forget. And even when you are gone, they are gifts that keep on giving.

CHAPTER 6

Exercise: The Fastest Way to Stay Young and Healthy

I have hated exercise all my life, and that is not changing now. Who originally invented exercise? Maybe God used it as punishment when he expelled Adam and Eve from the Garden of Eden. Especially as you get older, what other reason could there be for having to stretch and push your body into an unnatural form?

There is a reason. And the reason is that it is really a blessing! Exercise is meant to keep you moving and walking, without allowing rust to settle into your bones, joints, and brain. It prevents you from one day using a walker, or worse yet, a wheelchair.

Unfortunately, in my family, we have a sad example. Peter is now using a wheelchair because he cannot stand on his two legs. This could have been avoided, but he didn't think that moving and staying active applied to him. Even after a heart attack, he didn't follow doctor's orders to walk every day. When physical therapy was prescribed, he missed most of the sessions. Now, he is in a rehab facility where therapists are trying to strengthen his legs by having him exercise every day. We love Peter and are doing what we can to help him, but some of us say aloud, "All of this happened because he never moved." But now it is too late: Peter will most likely need a wheelchair for the rest of his days.

Move It or Lose It

As I said, I don't like exercising, but seeing Peter has made it clearer to me that it is a necessary part of daily life. Fortunately, there are many ways to stay active and to exercise. It is up to you to choose an activity that you feel comfortable with and enjoy, because if you don't, you won't do it for long.

No, a gym and treadmills are not the only answer; walking will do just fine. It will keep your joints supple and will even give your heart a good workout.

My neighbor Kathy, who is a painter, buys her paper and paints from Lee's Art Supplies on Canal Street. When it is time to go shopping, she walks from where she lives on 70th Street and Broadway to Canal Street and back, a distance of about five miles. She is eighty-two years old.

When I want to exercise, I dance. I put on some happy music with a nice beat and just dance around my living room for about fifteen minutes. It's enough to give my heart a workout. Besides making me feel alive, I am in a good mood for the rest of the day. If you feel a little silly when you first start, I understand—I did too. I wondered what I was doing by dancing around the room all by myself! But feeling alive and happy afterward will soon make you forget how awkward you first felt. Should you prefer not to dance alone, be like Marianne, who started tango lessons at age sixty-three. They got her moving, and pushed her out of her comfort zone and back into life!

Zumba dancing has become very popular, and it is hailed as a fun workout. It's so popular, in fact, that early morning classes are available for people to attend before going to work. My point is that dancing is a lovely way to exercise. No, you don't need to go to Zumba classes or a ballroom, or have a partner; you can do it at home, all by yourself.

Gym Guilt

Even when I was younger, I never joined a gym because I knew that I would never get my money's worth. Why not? Knowing me, I would have found lots of excuses for not going:

I am really too tired tonight.

I will go tomorrow.

And when tomorrow came:

Oh, I can't go today!

I have to meet Angela.

It's really too hot today.

I wonder if the air conditioning is working?

Excuses, excuses, but they all worked to keep me out of a health club.

But there are moments when I feel guilty for not going to a gym, like when I am traveling, and check into a hotel and the receptionist says, "Our gym is on the second floor, and it is open from six a.m. to ten p.m."

The offer is nice, but I came for a holiday, not a work-out. I know she has to tell me and means well, so I forget about it.

But when I go to breakfast in the morning and meet several gym-bound people in the elevator ready for the treadmills, I can't help but feel a little guilty that I don't put my health before the eggs and bacon that are waiting for me in the dining room.

So besides dancing, what do I do to stay fit? During my last checkup, the doctor asked, "Are you doing any exercise?"

I hesitated telling him what I was doing because I was afraid he would tell me it didn't count, or wasn't enough, or wasn't the right thing. I answered hesitantly, "Not really, unless walking up twelve flights of stairs counts?"

"Bravo," he said, "that is very good for your cardio-vascular system, and it will reduce your cholesterol. Just keep doing it."

I have to admit that I am not sprinting up those twelve flights of stairs. I have to stop at least twice to catch my breath, but when I reach the twelfth floor and I open the door to the hallway, I feel proud of myself.

You might only live on the fourth floor, but try climbing stairs daily because every bit helps!

Fool Them with Your Posture

A good posture can take years off how old you look. Pierre's sister, Asta, still took long walks with her dog every day until she was seventy-eight. Whenever I saw her, I hoped I would be like her when I became seventy-eight.

She was tall and slim, with very nice legs and a great posture. She walked with her shoulders back and her head held high, and from the back it was hard to tell how old she was.

"A funny thing just happened," she said one day after coming back from her walk with her dog, Pushi. "While walking along Spring Street, I heard a whistle behind me. You know, like the construction workers give the girls who are passing by? First, I didn't think it was meant for me, but when the young man on his bicycle passed me and looked at me with great expectations, I understood. Poor guy! He really got a shock. It was like lyceum from the back and museum from the front."

Always remember: the way you move and the way you carry yourself influences how old you look more than anything else. And this is not only true for the elderly; anybody with drooping shoulders, head bend forward, and not lifting their feet will look years older than they are—so walking straight, head held high and shoulders back might still get you a whistle, too!

Don't Let a Wheelchair Become Your Friend

One day, when arriving at the West Palm Beach airport in Florida, we saw a line of at least twenty wheelchairs at the exit of the plane, each with an attendant and waiting for somebody who couldn't or didn't want to walk. I didn't remember seeing any wheelchairs at La Guardia when we were boarding the plane, and I asked Pierre,

"Where do all these people needing wheelchairs come from? I didn't see them when we boarded."

He didn't answer my question, but said, "Let's just get out of here before they all come."

He was very uncomfortable seeing people in wheelchairs. I remember when we were waiting for friends in the lobby of our hotel in Bern, Switzerland. Suddenly, the three elevator doors opened, and plenty of wheelchairs came rolling out. Pierre watched them pass by and then said, "What is this? A wheelchair convention?"

I started laughing and couldn't stop for a long time. No, I wasn't laughing at the people in the wheelchairs, but at Pierre's face. He looked like he had seen ghosts; maybe he was afraid to be one of them one day? I don't know, but I have never forgotten his reaction, and when I see a wheelchair today, the memory still brings forth a smile.

The day came when my mother discovered the comfort of wheelchairs. No, she didn't need one, but she loved the attention she received when in one. When we were planning our trip to Florida, she said: "Make sure there is a wheelchair for me."

"Wheelchair? Why? You don't need one."

"How would you know? Just make sure there is one."

I made sure, and when we arrived at the airport in West Palm Beach, it was an especially busy day. A big, strong man appeared with a wheelchair.

"Just wait here," he said, once she was seated and strapped in.

We waited about ten minutes before he came back. All the while, my mother was getting more impatient. When he came back, he was pushing another wheelchair with a woman in it with his right hand, and he used his left one to push my mother's wheelchair. As they all started moving, my mother was indignant.

"How can you take us both together? That won't work."

"Relax, lady, we'll be at the taxi stand before you know it."

She really didn't care about getting to the taxi stand; her fun of being driven through the airport was spoiled.

When we came out of the terminal, I asked her, "You didn't forget to give him the tip, did you?"

"Tip? What for?" she said. "Pulling us like two old suitcases through the airport doesn't deserve a tip!"

That memory has not left me either, and when I pass a wheelchair in the airport, or anywhere else for that matter, I send a little thank-you to heaven for not wanting or needing one.

When he was close to ninety, Winston Churchill was advised by his doctor to exercise.

"Doctor, I get my exercise being a pallbearer for those of my friends who believed in regular running and calisthenics."

If you follow in Winston Churchill's footsteps, you won't know until you are ninety if you will be as lucky as he was. Personally, I won't take the risk and wait to find out. I am grateful for being forewarned, and having a chance to kick those wheelchairs way down the road and out of sight.

In a recent and widely watched YouTube video, Fauja Singh, from India, shared his story. When he was eighty-nine years old, he lost his wife and daughter, and to help him cope, he started walking. And then he started running and became the world record holder in his age bracket in the London Marathon, which he completed in six hours and two minutes. Today, he is 104 years old and still walks a few miles every day. He explains, "Being active is like a medication I don't want to stop taking!"

Therefore, telling yourself *I don't feel like exercising today*—and believe me, it happens to me often—is not an option because missing a day makes doing it tomorrow so much harder.

I usually overcome my inertia by taking a walk. A walk around the block, or walking instead of the taking the bus, it doesn't matter. Remember: every bit helps to keep the rust out of your joints.

Chapter 7

Don't Blame Your Age

"I tried to reach you last night, but you must have left already!" my son Marc said to me.

"What do you mean?" I asked. "We spoke when you were on your way home, before I left."

"Really? Oh! You are right! Just goes to show how I am on top of things."

Marc is young. And it is understandable that because of his work, his family, and everything else that is going on in his life, he forgets.

But there are no such excuses for me. If the situation had been reversed, my forgetfulness would have looked like a "senior moment." People think to themselves, "Can you believe it? She didn't remember that she spoke to me last night."

After Pierre's death was a very stressful time, and there were moments when I did not function well. I noticed surprised looks on my family's faces, like *Is she all right?* No. I wasn't, but not because I was going senile. I had trouble coping with my loss.

Another thing that happened at that time were disagreements about when and where we had agreed to do something. For example, "But I said eleven a.m., not twelve." In my fragile state, I didn't want to argue. Maybe I was the one who misremembered, but from that incident on I made all communications about time or place with my family and friends by email. And to this day, I keep the email in my inbox until the event has taken place.

There is no shame in forgetting, misunderstanding, or even being wrong, but what is wrong is that when you are older, your behaviors and idiosyncrasies are regarded as missteps due to your age.

Forgetfulness

This is at the top of the list. Don't let your forgetfulness get to you, and don't let anybody call it a *senior moment*. Just remember how many times your adult children, or other younger people you are in contact with, forget something! They brush it off with a casual, "Oh, I forgot," without fearing any consequences.

Last Mother's Day I was having lunch with my son and his family in Cafe Luxembourg, across from my building. Looking toward the door, my daughter-in-law Ann suddenly said, "Oh, there is Barbara from our building!" (We live in the same co-op, but not in the same apartment.)

I looked over and saw Debbie.

"That's not Barbara, that's Debbie."

She brushed it off with a short, "Ah, you are right." Nothing wrong with a slip of the tongue, but I was glad it wasn't my tongue that slipped.

And don't worry when you go into the next room to get something and you don't remember what it was when you get there. You are not losing your memory; you forget because you are not concentrating in the moment, and there could be another explanation, as Dr. Michael Ramscar of the University of Tubingen, Germany reassures us:

> Brains of older people are slower because they know so much. People do not decline mentally with age, it just takes them longer to recall facts because they have more information in their brains. Much like a computer struggles as the hard drive gets full, so too, do humans take longer to access information when their brains are full. Researchers say this slowing down process is not the same as cognitive decline. The human brain works slower in old age, but only because we have stored more information over time.[2]

Reassuring to know that your brain has not lost any of your knowledge or experience—it's just over loaded!

Repeating Yourself

I love this one. Who doesn't repeat themselves?

Armand, a good friend of mine in Switzerland, loved to tell stories.

"Did I tell you the story about the man I met a few years ago who works in the restaurant down the street?"

"Yes, you did."

We had all heard his stories many times.

---

2. www.seniorpsychiatry.com/docs/elderlybrains.html.

"Well," he said, "let me tell you what happened," and he would start telling his story. No, he wasn't hard of hearing or too old to remember that he'd already told us, he just loved telling stories, and we indulged him. But had he been older, this idiosyncrasy would have been seen as a result of his advanced years.

Yes, whether we know it or not, young or old, we all repeat ourselves. I try to avoid it by saying, "Stop, me if I've told you this already."

"Yes, you did," is often the reply, but there are times when I have the feeling my friends and family indulge me too. We all have stories we love to tell again and again. But you can be sure that has nothing to do with age!

Glasses

"Are you wearing glasses *now?*" Jill, my niece, asked me with great surprise.

"Yes, I am! I have to or I make mistakes!"

The other day when I had forgotten my glasses, I misread a coat check sign at the museum. The sign informed visitors that their liability was $200 for coats entrusted to them, but I thought it stated a $2 fee for the service. I was so embarrassed that I made myself a promise right there and then never to leave home without my glasses again.

But it happened once more, and I finally learned to wear bifocals, something I had resisted for years by saying they would make me lose my balance and fall. As it turned out, they don't! And what a relief it is not to have to look for my glasses when I am shopping in the supermarket. Now, I can see right away how much sodium is in the soup. *What? 700 mg!* And quickly put it back—high blood pressure, you know.

Today every optometrist offers an endless choice of frames in every shape and form to suit every face. And if you select the right one, it can even enhance your looks by adding a little mystery and interest to your appearance. So when the time comes and you need new glasses, pick a more fashionable style.

"How do you like my new glasses?" Jim asked (yes, men are vain too, more than women sometimes, I think).

"They are great, they make you look younger," I answered.

"That's what I need!" He laughed, having forgotten how bad he felt when he realized he needed stronger lenses.

Speaking of glasses, I can still see my grandfather (I called him Opa) sitting at the kitchen table repairing his own. One of the temples had come off. He always sat in his armchair next to the stove, except when he was doing something important like reading the *Offenbach Post* in the morning, or finishing a repair.

He was a quiet, shy man of few words. We never talked much, but, without words, there was an understanding between us I never felt again with anybody. He was tall and slim, with rugged features, light blue eyes, and a lot of white hair, making him look very distinguished and handsome.

Watching him, I asked, "Why don't you get a new pair?"

"Because there is nothing wrong with these once I am done with them."

If he didn't mind that he had to adjust them every few minutes because the wire he had used threw off the balance, he was right. He could afford to buy a new pair, but my grandfather did not believe in wasting things. Not money, not words!

But as we all know, wearing glasses is not only a matter of age. There are millions of people, including young people and even children, who need help to see. And if any woman thinks she is less attractive because she has to wear glasses, she is wrong—that time is long gone. Glasses are very helpful for hiding wrinkles and puffiness, and they can make your face more interesting, provided you stay away from rimless or scholarly looking styles.

In my survey for my book *What Turns Men On,* which appeared some years ago in *Penthouse* magazine, I asked the question, "Do you find women wearing glasses less attractive?" Eighty-four percent of the 6,000 men surveyed answered in the negative.

A twenty-nine-year-old freelance writer in New York wrote: "Emphatically no. On the contrary, the beauty of many women is enhanced by a nice pair of stylish glasses. They can decorate a face, because the lenses may serve as display windows for a fascinating pair of eyes. Glasses can also suggest an additional dimension to a lady's personality, i.e., intelligence, thoughtfulness, etc."

A twenty-five-year-old clerk in the army wrote, "Spectacles can even hold a hidden promise, and in no way do I find women wearing glasses less attractive. As a matter of fact, it looks sexy, especially combined with a bikini, because, with almost everything else uncovered, the glasses are hiding eyes that could be looking my way."

Other comments were:

"Glasses can make a woman look better, provided they are the right style."

"On the contrary, some women look beautiful with glasses."

"If they are fashionable and not horn-rimmed, they can be very sexy."

If you wear glasses or have forgotten your keys, or just don't feel like doing something, don't blame your age. These things happen to young people too—and they happened to us when we were young—so don't let anybody talk to you about having a *senior moment*.

CHAPTER 8

Every Cloud Has a Silver Lining

When you look for it, there is a silver lining to everything, even when you see your life slipping by. Knowing that your road ahead is not as long as the one behind you makes everything so much more precious.

At this stage of life, time is your enemy and your gift—an enemy because it shortens your road every day, and a gift because it makes you appreciate every day and everything in your life so much more.

Speaking for myself, I can see that I took many of my blessings for granted, thereby missing some of the best moments. Like the time when my son was growing up: I really had it all. I had a child, I had Pierre, my mother close by, and a business I loved. And I lived in my favorite city, New York, and a weekend house in the country. Buzzing around and between all of this, it never occurred to me that everything in life changes and that life wouldn't always be the same—and change it did.

Today, the child is a grown man. Pierre and my mother are dead, my business was sold, and the house in the Catskills burned down.

Some days, those memories make me feel nostalgic, but they also make me grateful for what is left and mindful not to miss anything. Above all else, they make me cherish each moment.

Having Choices

Luckily for you, with each additional year, not only your body changes, but also your thinking. I remember the day when I realized for the first time that I didn't think like a twenty-year-old anymore. It was a frigid, snowy winter night, when shortly before 10:00 p.m., my son, Marc, said, "I am going to the movies with Joe."

"What, now? At this time? It is snowing outside and very cold."

"That doesn't matter. We'll be all right."

Of course, they were. When I was his age, not even a snowstorm would have stopped me from doing what I wanted to do.

But as going to the movies on a cold winter night was no longer a priority, I was happy to stay in my warm living room watching TV.

When I hear somebody say, "I can't do that anymore," I always ask, "Do you mean you can't, or you don't feel like doing it anymore?"

There's a big difference! And being aware of this difference can change how good you feel about yourself. I would venture to say that most of the time when someone says "I can't do that anymore," what she really means is "Been there, done that—not on my program anymore!"

Not Sweating the Small Stuff

What a relief! I don't fret about the little things anymore. What does it matter when the dinner gets postponed to next week? Once upon a time, a change like that would have upset me terribly. I would think, *How could they be so inconsiderate and change the date at the last minute?* Today my reaction is, "I'll have something to look forward to next week!"

Not Working Anymore

Of course, when you are a senior, the biggest change is not having to work anymore, not needing to rush out of the house to be at the office at a fixed time. What a blessing and pleasure it is to sleep longer in the morning! I wake up without an alarm clock at 7:00 a.m. on the dot, and while hugging my pillow, I close my eyes again, feeling deliciously decadent.

Giving Back

"Giving back," or volunteering, has become the focus for many retired people, including me. There are days when I like to go somewhere to be useful, where they need me, where I will make a difference with pay or without.

There are many opportunities to be useful and make a difference by volunteering. And there's a feeling you get from giving back some of what you have learned in your long life that cannot be duplicated in any other way. But, as I found out, to be a happy volunteer you have to find your niche, a place where you feel appreciated, and above all else, where you feel that you make a real difference.

Everybody has a different niche, and finding your own is often a trial-and-error exercise. Let me tell you about my trials and how I finally found my spot.

When I had sold my business and there was no more office to go to, I felt like somebody had pulled the rug out from under my feet. That's when I understood what Pierre had meant when he said to me from time to time, "I am so grateful to you that I can be part of your business, because many of my retired colleagues have not even a stamp to lick."

Although he had been a chairman of the board, he now visited my clients to sell designs to the textile industry. I admired how he had adjusted. Yet until I was in the same position, I had not understood how important *being a part of something* is.

Not knowing what to do after I sold my business, I looked to my friends and wondered how they kept themselves busy. They went out for lunch or dinner, to the movies, to museums, or traveled. I joined them, but I still felt that there was something missing. For me, all these activities added up to what I call a Band-Aid, covering little scars but not the big hole that being retired left behind. I felt pushed out of the mainstream of life with nothing to do that was meaningful. And I couldn't be like my friends who said, "I am so glad that I don't have to work anymore and can just look after *myself* and do what I feel like."

When I first considered volunteering, I had to overcome a few obstacles that were deeply rooted in my mind. The first and most important was "I work for nothing." I had never believed in not being paid. The second one was "Volunteer work is only for people who have nothing else to do."

Putting those thoughts aside, I found out that it's not about passing the time or being paid, but about being useful, which is unquestionably necessary for a happy and healthy life.

Now, I volunteer at Bottomless Closet, an organization whose mission is to offer inspiration and guidance to disadvantaged New York City woman entering the workforce. We dress them appropriately for interviews, (the clothes are donated by individuals and clothing manufacturers), update their resumes, and coach them for upcoming meetings with prospective employers.

When after an hour and a half, Sylvia, a client (as we call them) walks out in her new clothes, her head held high and a smile on her face, the world looks like a better place. It is one where I can still make a difference. And when before leaving she hugs me and says, "Thank you, Brigitte, for finding the right clothes for me. I feel so good about myself now . . . and thank you for caring about me." I go home with my head held a little higher too.

When you cease to make a contribution,
you begin to die.

—ELEANOR ROOSEVELT

My Adventures in Volunteering

It took a few years and some trial and error before I found Bottomless Closet. It started with a visit to the Little Lord Museum in Berkeley Heights, New Jersey. I had passed it many times and wanted to visit, but it was always closed. One Sunday I got lucky; it was open. I stopped and went in.

The man on duty that afternoon introduced himself as Norman. He allowed me to walk alone through the farmstead, which had been built in 1760. It was a small, pretty farmhouse with most of the rooms still furnished. Everything in the place was dusty, and it looked like the dust of 1760 was still lingering. Cobwebs connected the windows with the once-white curtains, which were now full of holes. Before leaving, I asked Norman why it was not open more frequently.

"We don't have enough volunteers."

After a moment of hesitation, I asked if I could help.

"What would you like to do?" Norman asked.

"I could open the museum on another weekend, giving people the chance to visit. Or, if it would be all right with you, I could come and clean up and arrange the furniture a bit."

Norman thought that was a good idea. After a week of cleaning and rearranging with the help of my friend Donald, the Little Lord Museum had finally undergone a facelift. Donald, who was a photographer, took photos that, together with a story about the museum's history, were published a few weeks later in the *Independent Press*, the local community paper.

Norman liked what we had done, but when I asked him when he would like me to come and open the museum, he responded, "Actually we're fine. We don't want to open the museum more than once a month."

I gave him back the key he had given me, and left feeling depressed.

Back in New York, I heard assistance was needed at The Rocking Horse, my granddaughter Cosette's pre-school. For six months, I spent two days a week with little people, which I really enjoyed. However, the school closed down soon after because the owner could not renew his lease.

Then, I got more ambitious and thought of starting a nonprofit organization called "A Helping Hand," which would supply clothes to the homeless. With the help of my son, I went online and printed out forms—what seemed like a hundred of them. When I tried to fill them out, I got stuck very quickly, so I went to my accountant for help. Unfortunately, he crushed my hopes by explaining what was involved. I had neither the funds nor the help necessary to run such an organization. When I found out that I could not use the name "A Helping Hand" because it was already taken, I took it as a sign that it was not meant to be.

But the homeless were still on my mind. I found out that my church, the Holy Trinity Lutheran Church on Central Park West, has a program called H.U.G., which provides lunch and a few hours of companionship to homeless men and women every Saturday. I called and was told that they always need help preparing meals.

When I arrived on a blustery Saturday, the supervisor

met me, and after introducing me to six other volunteers, I was asked to cut lettuce.

While we were serving the meal, a lady named Patricia stepped up to the table.

"You wouldn't have a coat or jacket, would you?" she inquired. "I am so cold."

I asked one of the other volunteers if there were clothes somewhere. She pointed to a space behind a curtain, and that was where I found a few worn-out garments. Since Patricia was not a small size, all I could find to fit her was a men's jacket. I helped her put it on.

"This is a man's jacket, right?" she asked.

"That's all I have," I answered, feeling helpless.

"Well, it's better than nothing," she said gratefully, and, pulling it around herself, she walked out.

As I watched her, it hit me: they didn't need me to cut lettuce. They needed me to bring warm clothes.

Three weeks later, with the permission of the program's coordinator, Frank, I covered the two tables they had provided with a nice cloth and displayed the sweaters I had bought in a thrift shop (after many hours of weeding through racks to find the ones hardly worn, without holes or stains). They were arranged according to size and color, just as they would appear in a store.

I was a little apprehensive. Maybe they didn't want sweaters.

The first man stepped up to the table. "What is this?" he asked.

Frank stepped in. "If you need a sweater, help yourself. They are free. Brigitte brought them, and they are really nice."

"It's one per person," I told him.

He made his choice. Ten minutes later, he came back. "Can I change it?"

"Only if you have the receipt," I said. We both laughed, and he picked out another sweater.

After nearly two years of going to Watchung, New Jersey, every week to visit I.M. Unique, a thrift shop on Route 22, I ran out of funds, time, and energy and gave up on the H.U.G. Program.

Once again, I was without purpose. That is, until my friend Pat approached me one day.

"Somebody told me to donate my clothes to a place called Bottomless Closet. Do you know it?"

I didn't, but I looked up the phone number and then called to find out what it was all about.

"Would you like to wait for the next orientation evening or would you like to come in right away?" a friendly voice asked.

"I would like to come right away," I said. "How is tomorrow?"

"Tomorrow is fine. See you then!"

And the next day, I became a part of Bottomless Closet. Now, after being there for more than two years, I know I am at the right place. I use what I have done all my life—working in fashion and making women look better—to help people in need.

So if you are thinking about volunteering to feel happy, satisfied, needed, and useful, try to find a place where you can more or less apply what you have done during your working life.

Since it is not easy to meet new people in our ever-changing world, a rewarding and wonderful bonus of volunteering is making new friends—new friends open new doors, show you new places, and are like a burst of energy that enriches your life.

For Grandparents Only

Once you're a grandparent, your life changes. Your grandchildren are like a breath of fresh air. Christmas is again filled with magic and wonder. Birthday cakes have candles again, and parties bustle with little people running around, eating ice cream, and wearing funny hats. Vacations are not only for adult entertainment anymore; Mickey Mouse takes on a whole new meaning. And when it comes to shopping, every toy has your grandchild's name written all over it. When I see little dresses or anything pink, like sneakers with twinkling sparkles, I am overcome by an uncontrollable urge to buy them.

Thanks Heaven for Little Girls

I consider my grandchildren to be a blessing! They bring back memories of happy years, like when my son was growing up. And, if like me, you didn't have a daughter, a granddaughter—a little girl—is a special gift. But for me, having lost my own little girl when I was five months pregnant, she was more than a gift. It was like having a second chance.

Cosette arrived in the morning on a warm spring day in April. I had been prepared for hours to go to the hospital. The hospital was not far from where I lived, so I could walk.

It was nearly six o'clock in the evening when Marc called and said, "You can come and see her now." I was glad I could walk because I was too excited to sit in a bus or taxi. I walked as fast as I could, and chanted to myself, *It's a girl! It's a girl!*

I was thinking of my own little girl, and my emotions were tumbling all over the place. I was happy. I was sad. I was reliving the pain from so long ago, and I began to cry.

When I stepped out of the elevator in the hospital, I was greeted by the baby's brother, Remy, who was then four years old.

"Do you want to see my sister?" he shouted excitedly. "Her name is Cosette, and she has lots of black hair!" (When I had lost my little girl, the nurse was cruel enough to say, "You know, your little girl had lots of black hair.") He rushed ahead to show me where Cosette was.

I walked up to the plastic bassinet with my heart pounding—and there, wrapped in a white blanket, lay a little girl with lots of black hair nearly covering her pink face. Her eyes were closed, and she was sleeping. I looked at her for a long time, not daring to touch her, not hearing what anybody said.

For many years, I was not sure that I was going to be a grandmother. I had my son late in life, and as the years went on, I felt that my chances for experiencing a vigorous "grandmotherhood" were slim.

When Pierre was still alive and we started traveling to Florida, I was surprised to see many older couples waiting in the airport's arrival lounge. With great anticipation, they would look toward the doors where passengers came out. And when a little person came running toward them wanting to be hugged, I understood. After glancing enviously one last time, I would walk on.

Now, I have two grandchildren of my own. My grandson Remy, and my granddaughter Cosette—a *girl!*

She will be eight years old in a few months. And I am so grateful for having a little girl in my life. No, I have not told anyone why she is so special to me. But when we walk on the street, and I hold her little hand in mine, and she says, "Moma, you know what?" I feel so blessed for having a second chance, for being able to let go of the pain buried for so long.

But as grandparents, we can't get too involved. Our grandchildren do have parents, and they don't always do things the way we did. I was very surprised the first time I saw Ann take the baby's bottle out of the refrigerator and give it to the baby. I had the words "cold milk is not good for the baby's stomach" on the tip of my tongue, but I managed to control myself. Instead, I just wondered what had happened to warming the bottle and letting a few drops fall on the back of your hand to make sure the temperature was right.

I could go on and on about how differently we did things, but I won't. There are many roads that lead to

Rome, and from what I can see, my grandchildren are growing up just fine.

Another word of caution for grandparents: don't give up your own life. Making your grandchildren the center of your life is not healthy. Their interests change as they grow up, and once they are twelve (or even before then), grandma and grandpa are not as important anymore.

My mother made that mistake. Her family was the beginning and the end of her world. Her thoughts, attention, and her love, which was sometimes smothering, revolved around us, and especially her grandson. When Marc grew up and started his own life, she would often say, "I was good enough to look after him when he was little, but now he doesn't care anymore. He doesn't even have time to see his grandmother."

Of course, she exaggerated. When I tried to explain why he did not have as much time for her as she would have liked—that he now worked and had a family—I don't think she heard me. She felt hurt and left behind because the center of her world had moved on.

I have a friend (let's call her Mary) who is making the same mistake. She doesn't even schedule a movie or dinner outing unless she is sure her grandchildren can do without her that night.

To paraphrase Lotte Bailyn[3]: "Instant availability *with-*

---

3. Lotte Bailyn is the T Wilson (1953) Professor of Management, Emerita at the MIT Sloan School of Management. For the period 1997–99, she was chair of the MIT faculty.

out continuous presence is probably the best role a mother can play." True—and I think it applies to grandparents, too . . . maybe even more so. Think about it!

Let's Recap

The proverb *Every cloud has a silver lining* is usually said as an encouragement to overcome some difficulty. Yet, to overcome any negative situation, being positive makes that silver lining really shine, and for the road ahead your options have never been better. They are:

- **choices:** you can do what you please, when and where you please.

- **appreciation:** you know how to appreciate life.

- **relaxation:** you don't have to sweat the little stuff.

- **not working:** no nine-to-five schedule.

- **giving back:** a new satisfaction to make you feel happy.

- **grandchildren:** a new dimension in life.

- **last but not least, sex:** no fear of pregnancy.

CHAPTER 9

Is Paris on Your Bucket List?

When it comes to traveling, you should take the advice passed on by Anthony Bourdain, host of CNN's *Places Unknown*, who quoted Ernestine Ulmer: "Life is uncertain. Eat dessert first."[4]

Are you eating your dessert first? Many of my contemporaries say things like:

"I always wanted to go to Ireland."

"I have never been to London."

"It has always been a dream of mine to see Paris."

"Why aren't you going?" I ask them, and a list of reasons—I call them excuses—comes up.

"It's not the right time now."

"My grandchildren need me."

"I don't know. Maybe next year."

If you don't know now, when will you know? When it is too late? When your knees bother you too much to climb the stairs to the top of St. Peter's Basilica in Rome?

Traveling is one of the bonuses that comes with retire-

---

4. www.quotes.net/quote/34108.

ment. You now have the time to go somewhere for as long as you like. You don't have to be back because school starts, or because two weeks of vacation is all your company allots you.

I went on vacation with Marc and his family this year, and we had ten days to visit Munich, Germany. I felt happy to go, but I thought that ten days was not that much, and taking away two days for travel made it really only eight days. When we were booking the tickets, my son's question surprised me: "That's not too long for you?"

"Too long for me? No!"

"Well, old girl, this is the third act. What, if anything, do we have up our sleeve?"

I am so lucky now that nothing is too long. I have the luxury to do what I want, when and where I want. This is a wonderful bonus to what the French call *Troisieme Age* (Third Age).

Unfortunately, traveling is not as comfortable as it used to be. When I travel alone, the first hurdle is getting my ticket. No, I don't book online; I prefer to call the airline to speak to a human. I know there is an extra charge, as much as twenty-five dollars or more. But that is still cheaper than pressing the wrong button on my computer and paying twice, or going to the wrong place on the wrong day. (No, surfing online is not my forte.)

But even after speaking to a friendly, helpful voice on the phone, I still don't get an actual *ticket*. Remember those oblong, multiple-copy cards that showed all the details? Instead, the airline's reservation agent says she is sending me an email with my ticket information. When my son sees me print it out, he laughs and says: "You don't need that! They have you on file."

"They do? And if they don't, how can I prove that I have a reservation?"

"Stop worrying," he reassures me.

I admire his confidence in the system because I am not a trusting soul when my fate depends on a computer.

A few days before my departure, an email arrives from the airline telling me that I can print out my boarding pass, which will make the check-in faster and easier. Upon arriving at the airport, I am told the way to go is to put my passport through a scanner (which did not work at JFK on my last two departures) and to leave my suitcase "over there." They must be kidding—no way. I'd rather stand patiently in line and give my suitcase to a person who hands me my boarding pass and a receipt for my suitcase.

After my boarding card is in hand, I have to tackle the next hurdle: the security check. That's where we get undressed. Coats, jackets, belts, shoes, jewelry, and if the scanner shows a suspicious-looking object in my handbag, I am taken aside by a special agent who empties my bag. In the meantime, my other belongings are still being scanned on a conveyor belt, and are pushed around by the carry-on bags of other passengers. Once the agent is satisfied that there is only eye cream in the tube, I am free to go to find my other belongings. And while holding my shoes in one hand, with my coat and jacket slung over one arm and the rest of my belongings in my other hand, I look around for a chair where I can put myself together again. I'm a little irritated by it all.

"Traveling today is a pain in the neck," I hear my friend Debbie say. It certainly can be a pain, but going places is still better than staying home, don't you think?

Travel Solo or with a Tour?

Many people wonder about traveling solo or with a tour. Both have advantages and drawbacks, which depend on your age, relationship status, and how much comfort or adventure you seek. I have done both, and from my experience as a single woman, my advice is to go with a tour.

For my first trip when I was alone, I chose to go on a tour to Egypt. I had dreamed of seeing the pyramids ever since I saw a picture of them hanging in my classroom when I was only ten years old.

As we approached Cairo by air, the captain's voice came over the loudspeaker.

"Folks, if you look to the left of the plane, you can now see the Giza Plateau with the pyramids."

There was a rush to the left side, and "Oh, wow" came in unison from the passengers. In the distance, the late-afternoon sun made the three pyramids look like they were part of a Hollywood set. But they were not; they were real, and I had to swallow a few times.

After clearing customs, a representative of tour organizers Abercrombie & Kent met my twenty-one travel companions and me. They took us to the Hotel Freemont, near the Nile in the center of Cairo.

Our group was a nice mix of men and women who were young, old, and *very* old. One couple, Walter and Annie, were in their late eighties. They never complained about anything and went in and out of, or up and down, everything and everywhere. They lagged a little behind the rest of us, but they always made it . . . except one day when we had left the hotel in Cairo at 4:00 a.m. to catch a plane to Abu Simbel in upper Egypt, and then took another plane to go to Luxor, where we arrived around 4:00 p.m. and then boarded the *Sun Boat V,* a cruise ship that would take us to Aswan the next day. It was a steamy, hot afternoon, and they did not want to visit the Crocodile Museum, another site on our itinerary for the day. Instead they stayed on the boat, and so did I. We sat on the upper deck talking about our journey.

"Are you enjoying your trip to Egypt?" I asked Walter.

"I am—I mean—we are," he said. Looking at his wife for confirmation, he continued. "But we would have enjoyed it more had we come ten years earlier. We kept putting it off. Now, I just feel grateful that we are here."

Traveling in a group does slows things down, and often you can't see something that is not on the itinerary. However, not eating alone at night makes up for it, as I found out when I did travel alone.

Since my first trip to Egypt had been short—just ten days—and there was so much more to see, I went for another visit the following year, again with a tour. It was as fascinating as the first time, and when it was over, I felt I was ready to do it without needing the help of a tour guide, which would allow me to stay longer than just ten days.

So I prepared for my solo trip by booking hotels and sightseeing tours before leaving the United States. The New Memnon Hotel in Luxor[5], a recently built hotel facing the Valley of the Kings, was my first stop, and my first challenge. The owner, Mr. Sayed, was friendly and very attentive, but unlike on my tours, there was no welcoming dinner waiting for me, and worse yet, this hotel had no bar or dining room. Yes, they cooked breakfast and served it in the garden, but afterward, there was nowhere to eat, except for when Mr. Sayed offered to cook dinner, serve it on the roof, and share it with me. I declined. The nearest cafe was in the village and a taxi, which was not readily available, was needed to get there.

---

5. The New Memnon Hotel is a very beautiful, modern hotel, and the lack of guests during my visit was due to the collapse of the tourist industry after the 2011 revolution in Egypt.

After my first night, I learned I was the only guest in the hotel. I panicked, and then tried to stay calm. I asked Mr. Sayed where he and his family lived, thinking it was in the hotel.

"Down the street," he answered, "I will take you there and show you."

As I listened to him, I realized that I was stranded alone in a twenty-five room hotel, way out in the country-side of Egypt. I didn't speak the language, and I didn't have a phone. This is something that would have never happened if I'd been on a tour.

My salvation came when I called Sue and John, an English couple I had met on my previous trip and who happened to be in Luxor. After speaking to them, I took Mr. Sayed up on his previous offer to cook a meal and invited Sue and John to join me for dinner on the roof.

While we were eating, Sue turned to me and said in a firm voice, "You can't stay here. This is out in the middle of nowhere."

"But I have booked for ten days! I can't just leave."

"Oh, yes, you can. This is your holiday, and this is not where you want to spend it. You want to see people and have a drink."

The next morning at eleven o'clock, John came to pick me up and take me to the Pyramisa Hotel in the center of Luxor. I had paid Mr. Sayed for the ten days I had booked (it was only thirty dollars a day), and not wanting to hurt his feelings, I had told him that because of Hurricane Sandy, I was returning home early.

During the rest of my time in Luxor, Sue and John took me under their wing, which was better than any tour.

I admire Sue and John greatly. They have taken traveling to a whole new level. For the past seven years, they have been living in Luxor for six months of the year, from February to May and from October to the end of December.

"You really like Egypt, don't you?" I asked John.

"Many people back home ask me the same question," John answered, "and I always tell them, if we didn't go to Egypt, we would just be sitting around here with other older folks."

Spending part of their time in a different place from where they typically live has opened up a whole new world for them, and the challenges that come with it are wonderfully rejuvenating. But it would not be the same for a single woman. You need to be a part of a couple, especially in a male-dominated society like Egypt, where men deal with men. When Sue comes into contact with an Egyptian man, I love how she responds in an authoritative tone: "Oh, go and see my husband, Mr. John, over there. *He* will take care of it."

Maybe you are a part of a couple, or maybe you don't want to be away six months of the year, but then again, you should still consider doing something like this! Traveling opens new doors, and doing it part-time allows you to keep your world back home intact. You just put it on hold for a while. If you are not tempted by Egypt, online services like Airbnb offer very nice houses or apartments for rent in the South of France or Italy—or almost any-where in the world.

After my stay in Luxor, I went back to Cairo. I had another twelve days left before going home. I was staying in the Hotel Longchamps in Zamalek.

Zamalek is an affluent district of western Cairo encompassing the northern portion of Gezira Island in the Nile River. The island is connected with the riverbanks through three bridges. Years ago, many foreign embassies were located there in opulent mansions that still stand today.

The hotel was efficient (with a bar and dining room), and Doris, the German manager who had lived in Cairo for twenty-two years, was helpful whenever she could be. I spent my time in Cairo visiting the Cairo Museum again, taking a felucca (sailboat) on the Nile, walking through Old Cairo, and shopping in the Souk . . . and eating alone at night.

While still in New York, I had also made reservations for a two-day trip to Alexandria. Transportation, a guide, and a hotel had been booked. The Helnan Palestine Hotel at Montaza Palace Gardens was no disappointment. It had all the comforts one could hope for. It was located at the end of the Corniche, the waterfront promenade running along the Mediterranean, where luxurious mansions and exotic, grand hotels welcomed the rich and famous of Europe who were spending their summer vacations abroad in the 1920s.

My room, bright and welcoming, faced the water. When I stepped onto the balcony, the sight of King

Farouk's castle just a few hundred feet away, made me think that I had become part of *One Thousand and One Nights*. The beauty of the storybook-looking castle bathed in the rays of the setting sun, and the waves of the Mediterranean lapping against the rocks, made this a magical moment, but it was a moment I could not share with anybody because I was traveling alone.

What's my point? If you are single and traveling alone, a tour is your best choice. During those three weeks in Egypt, I never had a bad experience, but I learned that traveling alone is not as much fun as I had hoped, and eating alone at night feels very lonely. When you are part of a group, you might not love all twenty-one people, but there is always somebody you will bond with and share a table for dinner with.

The Beauty of Staycations

If you no longer want to deal with the hassles of traveling by plane or train or car, and faraway places are no longer on your bucket list, take a step back and look around you. Do you know your town well? Have you seen all there is to see?

I am the first one to admit that I am guilty of overlooking what is right in front of me. Realizing this fact, I have started to explore my city. Lectures and special tours, given by most museums, have brought new people into my life. Knowing about events that take place, such as concerts, discussions in the local library, and much more, makes me feel part of and connected to my surroundings in a comforting way.

"*We were thinking about the Himalayas this summer. On the other hand, there's something very special about Montauk.*"

Senior citizens make up most of the tourists traveling around the world today, and if you are not one of them, ask yourself why not. Isn't it time to fulfill your dream to see the Eiffel Tower?!

A New Approach to Traveling Is Needed

The rules of traveling change when we get older. Before every trip my friend Peggy Anne makes, she says, "I want to be comfortable, and I don't care about anything else."

Yes, it is nice to travel in comfort, but it comes with a price. However, when you check the details and do your homework, it is possible to get a good deal. And sometimes being comfortable is not only about money—here is a list of things that could make the difference:

- **Weather:** You don't want to be too hot or sightsee in the rain.

- **Prices:** There are certain times when you can find a real bargain—like hotels in London over the Christmas holidays—or if you book at the last minute, prices are greatly reduced because airlines don't want empty seats.

- **Hotels:** Especially when you go with a tour, ask for the name of the hotels you will stay in, and check them out online. The class of the hotel and the look of the hotel will tell you a lot about the quality of the tour.

- **Hotel location:** You don't want to take a bus or taxi to reach the center of town, and walking might not be an option, so make sure your hotels are centrally located.

- **Itinerary:** Read carefully, imagine yourself participating in an activity, and don't miss the small print. Taking a hike into the rain forest might sound wonderful, but can you hike for four hours? Do you even want to? Always consider if something might be a bit too challenging.

- **Flights:** Take only direct flights. Flying is not a treat anymore (do you remember when you got dressed up to take a plane?), and hanging around for hours at an airport waiting for your connection is not a *comfortable* start for a vacation.

- **Upgrade your seat:** There is a huge difference in comfort between steerage, as I call tourist class, and business. But if you don't want to spend the extra money, there is a way around it, as I found out recently while speaking to a booking agent of an airline. When you upgrade while checking in, the price of business class is reduced by 60 percent, meaning if the extra cost for business was $1,000, it is only $400 at check-in, which is much more affordable. As I said, airlines don't like empty seats.

- **Luggage:** Never travel with more than you can move yourself. There is nothing more frustrating than being bogged down by too much baggage. When you pack, remember that you can wear a garment a few times, and every hotel has laundry service that returns items the same day.

- **Take a tour:** Let somebody take care of you. Let them drive you, guide you, feed you, and best of all, your suitcases will come and go as if traveling by themselves.

Bon voyage and bon retour.

CHAPTER 10

"Did You Go Online?"

Going online is one way of staying connected to the world, and many elderly people who have computers (but there are many who don't) have learned to send emails, use Skype, and search on Google, but many others, like me, struggle.

No. I don't go online for information. It never enters my mind to do so, but that is always the first question Marc or Ann ask me when I need some information about anything—travel, products, places, history, people, the weather.

I don't know if I am glad I'm not from the "online generation" or if I would like to be. It doesn't really matter because I didn't have a choice. The Internet hit the world when I was past the age when it could have become second nature to me, like it is to my grandchildren today. I have learned to accept my shortcomings, but what still irritates me is that everyone belonging to the online generation looks at me as if I was left over from the eighteenth century.

Of course, there are exceptions among the elderly. Some of us have really stepped up to the plate and know all about computers. My friend Melissa's favorite phrase is, "Oh, I have to punch it up when I come home." Unfortunately, I am not punching it up, and everything I will say here is pretty much based on my ignorance about computers and/or my regrets that the world, the world before becoming elderly, has changed so fast, so drastically, that I can not follow all the way, all the time.

Yes, I have a computer, but I only use about 30 percent of its capacity. I don't know how the rest works or what it is for. Of course, I am writing this on the computer using Word, and it makes things really easy, but what is the purpose for all the other applications my son has installed? I am luckier than a lot of my friends who struggle with their online world because my son is a computer engineer, and I can call on him. Often I am too proud to ask because I think I must be able to fix the problem, but when I am not, which is most of the time, I call for his help. When he is not available, I call my thirteen-year-old grandson, Remy, who looks at me very seriously and says, "Don't worry Moma, I'll fix it—I'll be there in a minute."

Lo and behold, he does fix it. How innocent, how helpless, how ignorant children were when I was thirteen! Yes, this is a new world.

I know there are help sites on the computer where I can ask a question, and I have tried some of those, but when the answer comes, I don't understand what they are talking about. "Computer" is a different language that goes with having an online mentality, and it was not delivered with my computer.

Because I belong to the eighteenth-century generation, I'm surprised that getting information online replaces human interaction and personal knowledge. This does not

"I put in for reincarnation, but they said if you don't know computers forget it."

worry the online generation; neither does lacking personal knowledge, because knowing the Internet is there gives them all the self-confidence they need. It is their lifeline for everything. Who needs the *Random House Dictionary of the English Language* for spelling when there is spell-check?

When I ask Marc if I should buy a book about American history or any other subject for Remy, the answer is always: "No, all of that is online."

What happened to holding a book? I know the Kindle has taken over, and I have one, but I only read trashy novels on it because I don't want to see those on my bookshelves later. That said, the miracle of a book appearing on my Kindle screen within minutes after I have placed the order is not lost on me. But how is it possible to download so quickly? Everything to do with social media or the digital world is like a miracle to me simply because I don't understand how it works.

Take emails, for example. What a wonderful way to reach your friends, even if what you tell them is not private, as most people know by now. Speaking of privacy, Oprah Winfrey's advice might be helpful here: "Never write in an email what you wouldn't want to see on the front page of the *New York Times* the next morning."

Of course, not everybody heard Oprah say this, so the email archives must be full of things that would increase the *New York Times* distribution one hundredfold.

My friend Jeff, who is no youngster either, objects to email. He often says: "An email does not allow me to hear the tone of voice, which is sometimes more important than the message."

I think he has a point.

The World According to Facebook

Today, over one billion people are on Facebook. Are you one of them? If this trend continues, Mr. Zuckerberg will be ruling the world one day, much like a pharaoh in ancient Egypt.

"Are you on Facebook?" I'll ask somebody.

"Of course," they say. "I love that I can be in touch with all my friends all the time."

Once upon a time, we believed we were lucky if we had as many friends as we had fingers on one hand—that meant five. But today, we don't have enough fingers, even on both hands. Why is that? Because Facebook has changed everything—but for better or worse?

Both.

For better, because social media does connect the world in an unprecedented way. For worse, because you can't look your Facebook friends in the eye or give them a hug when they need one. No, it is not the same when you post the words "I am so sorry for your loss" on Facebook. A loss is made doubly painful by your physical absence.

Recently, I was sitting on my deck overlooking the garden with a cup of coffee. It was a beautiful, sunny morning. The grass was freshly cut. The soft breeze was moving the trees gently, singing its own song and making the world feel peaceful. It was a moment I would have liked to share with a friend.

Where are my friends? Don't I have any? Oh, yes, I nearly forgot—they are on Facebook. On that morning, I would have sacrificed all my friends on Facebook if I could have had one friend whose voice I could have heard.

No, I don't have many friends on Facebook (I think there are thirty-six), but I am repeatedly surprised by the self-indulgence and pride of most people who say, "You know I have over 300 friends." (Often, they have many more.)

When friend number 301 is found, there is a post that says, "Sally and John are now friends." How did they become friends? John lives in Sydney, Australia, and Sally in London, England. They have never met and most likely never will. I must really be out of the loop, because if I was Sally, I could only call John my friend if we had had a little history together, or had met at least once.

One of my friends on Facebook, let's call him Martin, has hundreds of friends—1,819 last I checked. He recently had a birthday, and—you guessed it—he received hundreds of "Happy Birthday" messages wishing him well. I think it is nice that so many people remembered his birthday . . . but did they really remember? They didn't have to because a notification appeared on Facebook to remind them. And there is no shame when a Facebook friend forgets your birthday. A few days after Martin's birthday, he received a post saying, "Sorry man, I missed your birthday, but I didn't check my Facebook for a few days—anyway, hope you had a great day."

I keep a birthday list, which I look at each month. I buy a card, sign, and send it, and when my friend holds it in her or his hand, there is a very special connection.

Could it be that the new way of being friends, of having so many phantom friends, camouflages loneliness and the lack of real-life friends . . . those people we can laugh and cry with?

By connecting you with so many people from all around the world whom you call friends but you have never met and probably never will, Facebook has found a way to change the word "friend" forever. What a terrible loss!

I am aware that the millions of Facebook members won't agree with me. They like to see what their friends are eating and how their children look (though it is not a good idea to have your children's photos out there). They delight in showing you what fun they are having when they play with their dog or cat. They never forget to post the happy photos during their vacation to brag about how wonderful the beach is and how luxurious the hotel is where they are staying. I look at it as a self–promoting, self–indulging tool—which, if not used wisely, can be very destructive.

Before I got off Facebook (yes, I did), I saw that Kevin, somebody I met once, had posted a photo of his wife Erika waiting for the bus. But really, who cares? I have nothing against either of them, but I don't care if Erika is waiting for a bus or riding in one. Is there nothing more interesting in his life he could have posted?

I got off Facebook for two reasons. First: I did not find most of the posts interesting, and therefore reading them was a waste of time. I email, phone, or visit my real friends. I don't need Mr. Zuckerberg looking over my shoulder. You might have heard that all information posted on Facebook is kept somewhere for eternity.

The other reason is the comments. They are often so abusive and outright disgusting that I don't need to be associated with people who claim to be educated yet use language and have opinions I wouldn't dare to repeat. I know, I don't have to read them, but if I don't, why be on Facebook?

Online Shopping

When it comes to shopping online, I am halfway there. Nothing beats Amazon when it comes to buying books, CDs, or household appliances. But when it comes to buying my wardrobe online, I don't think so.

When buying clothing, I like to touch the fabric, see the color, and try it on. I need to find out how I feel in it. I might need to try four or five dresses before I find the right one. My choices are limited when ordering online, and if I don't like something after it arrives or the fit is wrong, I have to put it back in the box or envelope, fill out the return form, make sure I keep a copy, and tape it all up. If I am lucky, the postal worker or the FedEx man will take it from our doorman, but if he doesn't, I have to make a trip to the post office or to FedEx. I find all that to be a real nuisance as well as time consuming. It is time I could have spent at Lord & Taylor while having fun trying on dresses.

This is another sign of my age, I know, because the online generation feels quite differently. They love online shopping. Reports about online retail show ever-increasing numbers. If I was a young mother, I, too, would appreciate that I could return my child's shoes to L.L. Bean without paying return postage, but then again, I am not a young mother. As I said before, my limited love for the Internet is due to the generation gap. I was not born holding an iPhone.

That said, I do have an iPhone now, and it is indeed very handy, with its many apps that help me live my life. I can pay bills, make appointments, locate the bus stop, look up stock market quotes, and perform hundreds of other functions I am not even aware of. However, I am waiting for the app they have not invented yet . . . the app that will make people look at each other—no, not on Facebook or Instagram, or Skype—but in person.

Intimate Connections

I was going home in the bus the other day and counted nineteen people holding their little square boxes, and I thought that if a naked woman would walk in just then, nobody would even notice. They were not just looking at their iPhones, they were completely immersed in them.

What will future generations do when they don't know what a real, flesh-and-blood person looks like?

It probably won't worry them because they are not used to seeing people in the flesh—instead they will see them on their computer, iPhone or iPad, or via Skype or other methods yet to be invented. A science-fiction novel I once read predicted that one day, due to sitting in front of computers, humans will have big heads and very short legs—no, not to worry, it was science fiction!

CHAPTER 11

People Who Need People

Barbra Streisand's voice has been sending this message around the world since she first sang the song in December, 1963. True then, now, and it always will be.

We all need people; we can't live happy lives by being alone. You need companionship from your spouse, friend, children, grandchildren, and the world. You need to share your feelings, love, and time. You need feedback to tell you who you are, to confirm that you are appreciated, needed, and loved.

For some time now, doctors and psychiatrists have agreed that we need to be engaged and have socially active lifestyles not only to be happy, but also to be healthy.

An article published by the Mayo Clinic, titled "Friendships: Enrich your life and improve your health," has this to say about the benefits of friendship:

> Good friends are good for your health. Friends can help you celebrate good times and provide support during bad times. Friends prevent loneliness and give you a chance to offer needed companionship, too. Friends can also:

- Increase your sense of belonging and purpose
- Boost your happiness and reduce your stress
- Improve your self-confidence and self-worth
- Help you cope with traumas, such as divorce, serious illness, job loss or the death of a loved one
- Encourage you to change or avoid unhealthy lifestyle habits, such as excessive drinking or lack of exercise.[6]

I have noticed that among the retired people I know, many of them became sick shortly after they stopped working and stopped having contact with other people.

It is not that they always felt great or were never sick while they were working, but by the time they reached the office, their minds did not allow them to feel any aches or pains. They had no time to dwell on them and soon felt better.

But after being retired and having too much time on their hands, they could feel every little pinch and pull.

It is nice not to have to be somewhere at 9:00 a.m., and getting up later is one thing I do enjoy so much. When I look out the window in the morning on a rainy day, and I have my cup of coffee while watching the news, I don't mind not having to go out. But I also know that if I didn't have much contact with other people, I would not feel well and become depressed. However, I don't let that

---

6. www.mayoclinic.org/healthy-lifestyle/adult-health/in-depth/
friendships/art-20044860?pg=1.

happen; on the days I don't do my volunteer work or meet
a friend, I make a point of going out, even if it is only to
the post office. Or I take a walk around my neighborhood
and end up having a glass of wine in a restaurant. If I
strike up a conversation with someone, I feel so much better when I go home.

There was a time when elder family members lived
with their grown children. For as long as I can remember,
my first husband's grandmother lived with them. She
helped with the household chores. She ironed the clothes,
prepared the dinner, and most important, she was always
there for the children. No latchkey kids in that family—
and who better to babysit than a grandmother? Speaking
as a grandmother, of course!

Today that connection is broken, and we are forced to
find new ways to stay connected, not only to our families,
but to the world at large. It's not easy. For some people it
might be outright impossible, and the result is that they
stay hidden away in their homes, and after a certain time
are afraid to go out.

A lady living in my building used to be a chatty, funny
character, but over time she became more and more with-
drawn and seldom said good morning. Now she never
even says that. One of the porters in the building told
me that they don't see her go out or ever see anybody visiting her.

When I picked up my mail the other day, she was at the
mailbox too. To my surprise, a young lady was talking to

her and telling her that she could pick her up tomorrow and take her to a concert if she wanted to go.

"No, I can't," the older woman replied.

"Why not?" the young woman asked.

She answered hesitantly, "I already have an appointment."

No, she didn't. The young woman did not believe her, but there was nothing she could say that would change the woman's mind. The older woman had lost all contact with the outside world, and going to the mailbox was the only time she saw another human being.

Maybe this is an extreme case, but when you look around, it is easy to pick out the people on the street who are lonely. With their heads bent down, they walk very slowly, not looking at anybody and often pushing a shopping cart. For some of these people it might be too late to find new friends and make new connections, but for many it is not, and you must be mindful to prevent isolation.

The first step is to stay in touch with your friends. Don't wait until they call you. Call them even if you have not heard from them for a while. My mother used to say, "If you wait for your friends to call you, you won't have any friends one day." My friendship with Marisa, who lives in Rome, confirmed this when she said, "If it wasn't for you, we would not be in touch anymore because I am not good at following up." I am glad I am because otherwise I would be missing our monthly telephone conversations, which keep us so connected, and which I very much look forward to.

When I found myself alone, I reflected on the words of my friend, Elaine, who had lost her husband a few years earlier: "It is very important now that you don't refuse any invitation. It will get you out there until you find your way." She was right. Whatever I did was not always my cup of tea. What I really wanted was to hold Pierre's hand, and it took a little while before I really believed that it would ever happen again. And often when I was out, I did not hear what the people around me were saying, but being in a room with other humans was better than the silence of my home.

Make Someone's Day

Quite by accident, I found a way to meet or start a conversation with strangers. It is easy to do and works every time—because everybody likes a compliment!

If you take a moment to look closely at the people you see—in a store, bus, elevator, or a restaurant—you can find something you can compliment them on. You will be surprised by how deeply you affect a total stranger when you smile at them and say, "I love your blouse."

Our busy pace of life, when we are always hurrying to get somewhere, has made people nearly invisible to each other. When I see a young, pretty girl walking on the street with her miniskirt and endless legs, and the men passing her don't even give her a second glance, I am happy that I was young when I was. Men paid attention then, and paying compliments to women was what they did best. Not so today! Maybe all the new regulations about sexual harassment have something to do with it. Who knows? But today it's women complimenting women.

When you first try paying someone a compliment, don't be put off by a person's stoic facial expressions; he or she will melt when you say they look nice, or you remark on a beautiful handbag. And if there is enough time, you will hear when, where, and how that beautiful bag was found.

When I entered the elevator the other morning, the young couple already inside did not acknowledge me in any way. They just stood there looking grim and preoccupied. Once we reached the lobby, the woman began to walk out, and I looked down at her shoes. They were spectacular—black suede, with five-inch heels and lots of cut-outs and fringe. Walking behind her, I couldn't help myself and said, "Oh, wow, your shoes are so beautiful. I really admire how you can walk in them."

She turned around, and I thought it was a different woman. With a big smile on her face, she answered, "Thank you! You think they are beautiful?" She laughed and pointed to the car that was waiting by the curb. "But you are mistaken," she continued. "I can't walk in them. I can just make it to the car."

She made it to the car and waved good-bye; we both started our day with a smile.

If I have not convinced you yet, let's put the shoe on the other foot. Think about how you feel when you are complimented on your looks, or on what you wear, or on something you did. You might even come home and tell your husband, "Guess what? There was a lady in the supermarket with me this morning who complimented me on my hairstyle."

Yes, it is very powerful and uplifting to be noticed and praised. It strokes your ego and makes you feel better. So why not return the favor and acknowledge what is good, let others know what you like about them, and make them feel special?

CHAPTER 12

Mirror, Mirror on the Wall

When it comes to your appearance, a mirror is really your best friend. A friend you can trust, who tells the truth, without criticizing or flattering you.

The mirror known today was invented in 1835 by a German chemist, Justus von Liebig. But the human need and desire to see what we look like goes back 8,000 years, when in Anatolia, mirrors were made of ground and polished volcanic glass.

What makes us want to see ourselves? Is it because we want to compare ourselves with other humans? Is it a self-confirmation? Or is our vanity hoping to confirm that we are the fairest of them all? Whatever the reason, we can't imagine living without mirrors.

An old, homeless man sitting on the sidewalk in front of my house stopped me one day, and, assuming he wanted money, I bent down to give him a few dollars.

"No, thank you, I don't want your money, but could you be so kind as to get me a mirror? I haven't seen myself for a long time."

My first reaction was that there are mirrors everywhere,

but when I looked around my neighborhood, to my astonishment, there were no public mirrors. Store windows do not allow people to see themselves properly, and the homeless are typically not welcomed into places where there are mirrors.

When I gave him the hand mirror I bought for him, he looked at himself for a long moment. Then, while putting it carefully into his pocket, he smiled and said, "God bless you!"

I felt blessed. He had just taught me a lesson: how vulnerable and lost I would be if I couldn't see myself.

Aging Beautifully

Unfortunately, as you get older, you don't usually become prettier, and to look good, you often have to work a little harder. Some days, even a lot harder. I call it the "stretch, dye, bleach, lift, tan, and stimulate" phase of your life. You exercise, dye your hair, go to tanning salons, bleach your teeth and brown spots, pay for Botox injections, or go for cosmetic surgery like a facelift.

Have you had one? I wouldn't mind having some of my wrinkles disappear, but I am afraid of knives, and I promised Pierre I would never have a facelift because he always loved me the way I am. But now that he is gone, some days I wonder if I still have to keep my promise.

"She had some work done, you can tell," women whisper as they look at other women. Indeed, many have had some work done. But if you can't see it, why should you have it done? Maybe it is so obvious because doctors seem to have a look-a-like model that they apply to most women. It is the doll-faced look, where the cheeks are round and pulled up, the eyelids hardly move, and the full lips and skin are shiny and stretched tightly over the bones. But then again, a pretty doll is better than a rag doll.

"Have you ever been young before?"

As I said, I am afraid of knives, and after helping my friend, Elli, suffer through a neck lift, I am even more scared. The surgery took much longer than anticipated, and when I went to pick her up, I found her in a dark recovery cubicle.

Oh, my God what has happened to her? I thought. She couldn't talk because her face was heavily bandaged from her chin to the top of her head. She was moaning, and when I asked her if she was in pain, she nodded and gestured with her hand that I should find the doctor. He came and asked, "What's the matter?" Elli did her best to communicate that she was in terrible pain, to which the doctor replied, "Okay, I will give you some more painkillers."

We sat for a while, waiting for her to feel better, and when we went downstairs to catch a cab, I was wondering how I would get her home.

She stayed with me for the next two days. She was in pain most of the time.

"If I had known that it would be like this, I would never have had it done," she said.

It took several weeks to heal, and during this time she had to wear a chinstrap at night, but after all those weeks and all that pain, her neck looked much better than mine.

Comparing my neck with Elli's, I really didn't like mine anymore.

The next time I went to see my acupuncturist, which I do every three months for my circulation, I asked her if she could do something about my neck.

"No, acupuncture doesn't go that far, but have you heard of Thermage?"

I looked into it. It promised to give an overall younger-looking appearance by using radio frequency energy to tighten the collagen in the skin, thereby filling out wrinkles and fine lines. It is marketed as a single treatment, with no pain and little-to-no downtime.

I went to see a doctor on Fifty-Seventh Street for a consultation. He explained that the procedure would take about two hours and that the effects were not immediately visible, but that in a few weeks, I would see a difference. After I had the procedure done, I found that what the doctor had told me was true. About a week later, my skin started to look healthier and plumped up, and my neck was better, too—but not as good as Elli's. "No pain, no gain" must be true!

An Alternate Choice

Many years ago I read an article in *Cosmopolitan* magazine about Carol De Maggio. Although Carol was only in her thirties her husband thought she was aging prematurely, so she developed a program called *Facercise*. A program to exercise your face—why not? You exercise your body, right? In Carol's words, "A muscle is a muscle to be exercised."

Your face has fifty-seven muscles, and her program has fourteen exercises to be done twice a day. By working these muscles, the skin tightens and blood circulate through your face, making your skin look fresher and the muscles lifted.

After reading the article, I bought the DVD and have done the exercises ever since, and I am sure it has slowed things down. Of course it is like all exercise: You must keep it up to have results. How do I know? Because when sometimes I stop for a week or so, I can see a change. The exercises take only fifteen minutes a day. And no injection, knives, or pain.

Maybe Facercise is something you would like to look into. How expensive is it? About fifty dollars for the DVD, and less for her book (which I don't think is really needed if you have the DVD).

But when all is said and done, I think it is wonderful that we don't have to live with a wrinkled face if we don't want to. Yes, we have all heard that wrinkles give character to a face—or that we have earned our wrinkles—but my question is *Couldn't God have offered a better reward than wrinkles for leading a long life?*

Since modern society has created the cult of youth worship, which is hard to get away from or ignore, everyone at one time or another has probably played with the idea of "having work done." Some of us have stepped forward with great courage and now look ten (or even more) years younger.

A coworker of mine had a pleasant, unexpected, and wonderful surprise after her own surgery.

"Did you know, since I went under the knife, young men are propositioning me. I don't know how to handle it. Sometimes I feel I could be their mother."

"Don't handle it," I said. "Enjoy it!"

She never told me if she took my advice!

Facelifts and corrective measures are not undergone only by women over sixty. Many much younger women start way before it is necessary.

"I just had some Botox," my neighbor, who is only forty, told me when I met her in the hall the other day.

"But you are still young. You don't really need it."

"Sure I do. I can't stand those lines on my forehead, not to mention the little wrinkles around my eyes. Doesn't it

"*Botox.*"

look good?" she asked. I nodded and thought, *How will
she look when she is my age? How will her skin be after years
and years of treatment?* Perfection is great, but it can be too
much of a good thing if it isn't handled correctly.

I don't know if I will ever have a facelift. Maybe I can
live with the character the years have given my face, but
when the day comes and my "mirror, mirror on the wall"

no longer shows me what I want to see, I am glad I'll have a choice.

Should *you* ever consider having plastic surgery of any kind, do as much research as you can. Go online. Consult with different doctors in person, and remember, the best reference you can get is from a woman who had some procedures done (who looks great). Ask for the name of her doctor, and consult him.

When Dolly Parton was asked during an interview if she ever had any plastic surgery done, she laughed and said, "There is nothing wrong with a little tuck here and a pull there!"

And she looks good! Maybe we can get the name of her doctor?

CHAPTER 13

Enjoy What You Eat and Drink

"**O**h, I shouldn't, but they are so good," Monika said, picking up a second cookie.

"It's only the second one, and why shouldn't you?" I asked.

"I am trying to lose weight, and you know my cholesterol, I have to be careful."

If you are like most of us, you have become so programmed (or brainwashed) to eat healthfully that food has become forbidden fruit. No doubt your stomach is not what it used to be, and you might have to be careful about how much you eat or decide whether that huge steak is something your stomach and arteries can still handle.

During a recent dinner party celebrating the birthday of Henry, the friend of a friend of mine, I saw firsthand how one can (but shouldn't) handle cholesterol. When Henry's twenty-four-ounce steak arrived, he took a little box out of his pocket and popped a pill. Looking at us, he explained, "Cholesterol, you know," and then he swallowed the pill. "Now I can enjoy my steak," he added and dug in.

Marc and his family do all the right things. They exercise, avoid fatty food, eat almost no meat, and abstain from coffee and alcohol, and they tell me that how you take care of yourself when you are young will determine the shape you are in when you are old. I am sure that they are right, and listening, I really wonder why I am still here, because I did all the wrong things when I was their age.

Whether we were at home or traveling around the world, we ate everything, never asking if it was good for us; we just enjoyed it. We drank wine and had a few martinis before dinner. And on vacation in Spain, the Spanish cognac helped digestion and made the evening stars shine brighter. What fun it was!

Do the youth of today enjoy their food and drink? I don't know, but I can't imagine that green tea does the same for you as a glass of good wine.

Importance of Water

Oh, I still love and drink wine, but I have learned how important water is for my body, skin, and digestion. Not that that makes me like it, but I drink it—when I don't forget.

Whenever I visit my son, my daughter-in-law hands me a big glass of water as I walk in the door. Sometimes, I wish it was wine, but it never is. They live a healthy lifestyle, remember? Genie, a girl I worked with who also didn't like water, used to say, "If God wanted us to drink water, he would have given it some taste."

But this obstacle has been overcome. The soft drink industry now offers us water with many different flavors. So my excuse of not liking water because it has no taste is not valid any longer!

Healthy . . . and Happy?

When my first husband, Jacques, and I arrived in the United States many years ago, food was not an important topic in America. Wonder Bread was the only bread there was, and it was hard to eat. We were used to French baguettes. Before coming here, we had lived in Paris, France, Jacques's hometown.

Julia Child's cooking program on television was the first breakthrough in changing the way we cook and eat today, and her raspy voice even seduced children. It was my son's favorite program when he was only three years old and didn't yet understand the meaning of *boeuf bourguignon.*

Today, magazines are filled with recipes and advice for how to cook and what to eat to stay healthy. The many food channels on television all battle for your attention. Clicking the button on my remote control, I get one station after another where somebody is preparing a meal, which makes me wonder, *Have we just invented cooking?*

The thousands of books, articles, and even workshops about how to stay healthy and become centenarians (of which there are thousands in the United States today), never seem to forget us. They are like the cooking channels, and I am sure they all give good advice, but I want to tell you about a few people I have known, or read about, who did not follow all the rules, became very old, and had a lot of fun doing it.

A French television reporter interviewed two sisters who own a beauty salon in a small town in northern France. One was ninety-two years old and her sister was ninety-four. When asked why they were still working and how they stayed in such good shape, one sister said, "What else would we be doing? Sitting at home, watching TV, and drinking too much?"

"Why do you think you became so old?" asked the young man who interviewed them.

The sisters looked at each other with conspiratorial smiles. Pointing to a bottle of Remy Martin (a popular French cognac) on the table, one of them said, "Because every night before going to bed, we have a glass of that!"

While refilling her bowl with another few scoops of ice cream, Barbara, who is now in her late eighties, said, "I think I am old enough now to have earned the right to eat what I want and not worry anymore about how good it is for me."

Angelina, the mother of my friend Marisa, who lives in Rome, just turned 104. She refuses to take any medication beyond a sleeping pill now and then, and she still cooks and eats whatever she feels like, including a glass of wine.

Marie, Pierre's mother (who was Belgian), liked the good life, especially when it came to food and drink. Like most Belgians, she was known for being a gourmet and she was one in the truest sense of the word. At seventy-eight, she had some heart problems and was told not to drink, and definitely not to smoke, which she had been doing since she was fourteen years old. She listened, stopped drinking her bottle of champagne each evening, and cut out the cigarettes. But life was not the same. She felt deprived and depressed. So one night, after five years of abstinence, she asked her grandson, Andre, to go out and buy a bottle of champagne and a pack of cigarettes.

"Are you sure?" he asked.

"Never more than today," she said. "I know I will die, but until then, I don't want to miss what I love."

She lived drinking champagne and smoking her cigarettes for another ten years. Maybe she knew something we didn't until now. The article, titled *"Drinking Champagne every day could help prevent dementia and Alzheimer's,* gives me hope.

In news that both offers hope and baffles, scientists have found that drinking three glasses of champagne every day can help to prevent the onset of Alzheimer's and other forms of dementia. A compound found in pinot noir and pinot meunier, the black grapes used to make a bottle of the fizzy stuff, can ward off brain diseases and increase spatial memory.

Professor Jeremy Spencer—one of the academics who carried out the experiment involving rats at Reading University—told the *Mail on Sunday* "the results were dramatic."

He continued: "This research is exciting because it illustrates for the first time that moderate consumption of champagne has the potential to influence cognitive functioning such as memory."

Those who conducted the study now hope to move on

to trials involving pensioners. Meanwhile a spokesman for the Alzheimer's Society described the results as "interesting", but added: "A lot more research is needed." We await more news with glass in hand . . .[7]

I think that a life without fun, without some small pleasures, is a life of poor quality. And if a piece of cheese

"Damn it, who ate all the chèvre?"

---

7. www.townandcountrymag.com/leisure/drinks/a4269/drinking-champagne-dementia-alzheimers/.

and a glass of cognac or champagne in moderation is all the fun you can have, so be it—even if the life you live is a little shorter.

Woody Allen once said, "You can live to be a hundred if you give up all the things that make you want to live to be a hundred."

In Germany, I found an antique porcelain plate from 1880. It has been hanging in my kitchen for many years, and it sums up this idea best:

The Best Doctor Is Always
Your Own Sense of Moderation

CHAPTER 14

Staying Slim and Trim

If you think you have a few extra pounds you could live without, consider this question: Would you really like to be skinny? It would mean more wrinkles in your face. Or would you like fewer wrinkles but a few extra pounds around your waist? This is a difficult choice and one that only older women have to make because young women have no wrinkles anywhere.

To check if I am right, look at heavier women's faces. Do you see that they have fewer wrinkles? Now, look at a woman you have just admired for being so slim. Unless she has "had work done" (as the expression goes), she will have a more lined face.

So what do you go for? If you want to be skinny, let me mention an article that appeared in *AARP Magazine* about the advantages of a few extra pounds in the event we get sick or need an operation. It stated that extra pounds give the body a better fighting chance. Not only is that an incentive not to be too skinny, but it is permission to have a second cookie. How about that?

Ten Commandments for Staying Slim and Trim

The women in our family were not slim. They were all on the plump side, including me. The extra pounds were a problem when I started modeling. I went on diets and ate very little. It was very difficult because I love to eat. Sometimes, I felt that just looking at food made me gain weight.

I became slim enough to fit into the skinny clothes that were being photographed for the next catalogue spread, but I never reached the frail waif look of runway models, and consequently because I was not skinny enough, I missed out on a few assignments.

During this time of deprivation, and later when I was not modeling anymore and didn't want to become plump again, I came up with what I call the "Ten Commandments for Staying Slim."

This is not a complicated, forbidding diet. It only requires common sense, which, if applied correctly, works like a charm without penalties and failures, and without making you feel guilty for taking a second cookie. Most important, it is not harmful to your health. You will get great results if you follow this plan. (This has all been said before, but reminders never hurt.)

1. **Never say "diet."** Instead, think in terms of moderation. Being on a diet will make you feel like an outcast, and when you say you are on a diet, everyone takes a second look to see how heavy you are. Listen to Oscar Wilde, who said, "Everything in moderation, including moderation."

2. **Never skip meals.** Yes, you must have breakfast to

kick your metabolism into gear, and if you miss other meals, you will be so hungry that you will eat more than you should at the next meal.

3. **Never eat an appetizer and a dessert.** Just settle for one or the other.

4. **Never take seconds.** Regardless of how delicious something is, as mentioned before, it is important to practice moderation.

5. **Never eat between meals.** The little between-meal nibbles eventually become the extra pounds.

6. **Halve your portions.** It is not what you eat, but how much of it, that makes the difference.

7. **Don't eat while cooking.** Of course, you have to taste what you're preparing, but not too often or too much. Otherwise, it is the same as increasing the portion of the meal you will eat later.

8. **Eat only when you're hungry.** It might be time for a meal, but don't eat if you are not hungry. Don't let the clock dictate your eating habits.

9. **Write down what you eat.** Many people say "I don't eat much," but seeing it written down might surprise you. Generating a list will show you where you can cut down on calories.

10. **No exceptions to the rules.** Don't find reasons to make an exception. Yes, they are easy to come up with:

- "It's the weekend."
- "I feel depressed."
- "I feel lonely."
- "I was invited to dinner."
- "My mother is coming to visit."
- "I have a birthday party."
- "Christmas is coming."

I am not saying there is never a time for an exception, but it should be reserved for a very special moment. When you eat more one day, it is harder to eat less the next day.

The most important and effective rule is Number 6: Eat less.

It is well known that in France there are very few overweight people. What is their secret? Small portions! I still remember my first visit to my future husband's French family. My mother was with me, and when we sat down to dinner, there were nine people around the table. Each meal always included several courses, starting with hors d'oeuvres.

Nadine, my future mother-in-law, brought in a huge platter with a small, and I mean *small*, square (six by six inches) of pâté. I looked at it and then at my mother, and I knew we were both thinking the same thing: *This can't possibly be enough for so many people!*

Not only was it enough, but there was a piece left over after everyone had been served. This was my first culinary lesson in my new country: big dishes and small portions.

Losing and keeping off the few extra pounds will make you:

- feel more energetic,

- feel more confident,

and

- your clothes will fit better,

- it will be easier to shop for a new wardrobe,

- you won't ever have to say "I'm on a diet," and finally,

- you will like yourself better!

CHAPTER 15

Makeup: Less Is More

$\mathcal{G}$ still remember the time when makeup made me feel and look glamorous. In contrast, today I must apply it with great care to avoid showing off the wrinkles. My biggest help in avoiding this (as much as possible) is a magnifying mirror.

Wrinkles on Steroids

Oh, believe me, there are days when I would rather not be looking into a magnifying mirror because it shows every little line and discoloration, mercilessly highlighting the dark circles last night's party left behind. The other day when looking into my magnifying mirror, I saw my larger-than-life wrinkles, and I had one of those "oh no!" moments, and I only felt better when I remembered that others don't see me quite so magnified. When I turned the mirror around to the normal side, I was happy to see that all my wrinkles had shrunk!

By using a magnifying mirror, you will apply your makeup to the right place without dabbing on too little or too much. I knew a lady who told me that she had put hers away because she just couldn't stand to look at herself—a pity. With a few minutes of suffering, her mascara would have been on her eyelashes instead of halfway up her eyelid. And she would have seen that her eyebrows were not the same shape.

I am not a beautician or a makeup artist, but I have learned that even though the years are increasing, my makeup has to decrease. I am sure we have all heard *less is more,* though maybe there are women who have not? Otherwise, why would they let foundation sink into their wrinkles and make them more visible?

Enough criticism! As I said, I am not a beautician; I am just sharing what I found to work best at this time in my life.

Good Skin

Women who inherited their mothers' good skin are lucky. But if you haven't, there is still a lot you can do to have healthy looking skin. It starts with moisturizing and then moisturizing again. I never stop putting moisturizer on my face and body. Sometimes I think my middle name is "Moisturizer," because when I get up at night, especially in the winter when the air is dry, I put moisturizer on my face before I go back to sleep. It is right there on my night table.

But if you don't get up during the night, there is a simple, effective way to hydrate your skin while you sleep. When years ago, I saw for the first time little lines and wrinkles around my eyes, I panicked—*What are those?* I wondered, *Where did they come from? No, not me! Not yet!* I shared my sorrow with my friend Corinne, who was a model too.

"Do you have a humidifier in your bedroom?" she asked.

"A humidifier? No, what is that?" I inquired.

After she explained that it can keep your skin moist and prevent dryness, I bought one, and it worked. Since then, I don't go sleep without it, especially in the winter when the heating dries out the air. I switch it on about two hours before going to bed so the dry air has time to dissipate, and when I get up my skin feels smooth.

When you are not sleeping, the best way to moisturize is to drink plenty of water throughout the day. The amount of water in the human body ranges from 50 to 75 percent. If you fall below that, it will affect how soft and smooth your skin is.

And moisturizing extends to your body. Applying a moisturizer after every shower or bath will make you soft all over. A lot of women stop moisturizing at the neck. Instead, include your décolleté. It's as important as your face, so make it a part of your routine when applying moisturizer.

Tanning

The kindest and best thing you can do for your skin is to stay out of the sun. This was true even when you were younger, but even more so now because your skin is more sensitive and thinner than in the past. Sunbathing is not recommended at any age, but despite the dermatologists' warnings about skin cancer, most of the world still wants to be tanned.

There was a time when just the opposite was true. In the nineteenth century, upper-class women used parasols and wore long sleeves and hats to prevent the sun from affecting their pale complexions. But this all changed when, in the 1920s, the French fashion designer Coco Chanel accidently got a sunburn while vacationing on the French Riviera. When she returned to Paris, her fans liked her look, and the tan as we know it was born.

During the Industrial Revolution, which took place in the eighteenth and nineteenth centuries when agrarian rural societies in Europe (and America) became industrial and urban, being tanned meant that you could afford a luxurious lifestyle of vacationing in the sun.

Hats—Decoration or Protection?

Hats are worn for many reasons—ceremonial, religious, safety, fashion—but when it comes to the sun, there is only one reason—to protect our faces from its harmful rays. And besides this useful purpose, a hat can make a fashion statement. There is nothing more flattering than a straw hat with a large brim, and adding a pair of fashionable sunglasses completes a movie-star image.

But if a hat makes you feel hot, a parasol is a good alternative. Most travel catalogues and stores selling vacation gear also sell parasols (sun umbrellas). A parasol not only covers the head but also the upper part of your body, allowing you to feel the breeze. And don't be tempted to use your rain umbrella because the fabric they are made of will intensify the heat and the rays of the sun.

The desire to be tanned is often pushed to the extreme. A very dark tan is aging, and so is leathery skin. To avoid this you should never be outdoors without sunscreen—

an ingredient found in most moisturizers and foundations today.

Today, beaches and poolsides are still filled with sun worshipers who expose their bodies to the damaging rays for hours, and when from time to time they turn over, I can't help but think of a piece of meat being grilled. When a woman is topless and I see her breasts exposed—well, you can imagine what that makes me think of—sunny side up or over easy?

Unfortunately, it is not always the woman with the best breasts who is topless. I remember vacationing in Marbella, Spain, which is a popular holiday destination for German and English vacationers, when Marc was seven. One day while walking along the beach, he suddenly stopped and stared at two women sunbathing. They were topless, and their heavy breasts were not only enjoying the sun but also the freedom of being loose!

"Don't stare, come along!" I said, pulling him away, but his head was still turned. It was his first time seeing bare breasts, and he has never forgotten it.

But I am getting away from the subject of tanning. I like to be tanned. I don't like my very pale, white skin. Since the sun is not my friend, I have found another friend: a self-tanning product that works very nicely. It works so well that I am often asked, "Oh, where did you get your tan?" Nobody knows it's out of a tube!

There are many products on the market made by well-known cosmetic companies that will give you a nice tan. I use Jergens Natural Glow (fair to medium). I apply it after a shower or bath on well-dried skin. Using it once a week is enough to give me the tan I want.

When you buy it for the first time, pay attention. Choose the shade that is best suited for your skin (there are shades for all skin tones), and when in doubt, start with a lighter shade. Don't use too much of the product, and most important, rub it in well and evenly, just like your moisturizer. If you follow the directions properly, you will see your skin take on a lovely glow.

Foundation and Concealer

What pantyhose do for legs, foundation and concealer do for your face. These products subtly hide imperfections and take away the bareness. I use concealer around my eyes and to cover my brown spots. Then, using a soft brush, I gently cover my face with a powdered mineral foundation (this product generally has sunscreen in it, too). If applied with a light hand, it does not look like you are wearing powder, which is admittedly a look of the past. It also does not highlight wrinkles like many of the liquid foundations do because they settle into the creases, which makes them more visible.

My grandmother's final touch to her morning toilette was a dash of powder on her nose—just the nose. "A shiny nose shows lack of class," she would explain.

I loved the smell of the powder. It was of the palest pink one can imagine. She kept it in a small, round silver box that stood on the credenza in the combination kitchen-living-dining room. Sometimes when she was not looking, I opened the box carefully and inhaled the smell, daring to put my pinky in it to try and catch a little of the magic. Today, that little silver box stands in my bedroom. Some of her powder is still in it, and the magic is still there.

Her name was Katherina, a name that befitted her regal composure and her belief that she was not like everybody else. She was tall, not slim, but not heavy either. Her body was dominated by her bosom, from which her figure went straight down to her long, shapely legs. During the week, she wore cotton dresses protected by an apron with big pockets to hold her ever-present handkerchief. She wore her gray hair piled up on her head, only taking it down once a week to wash it. When she thought a little extra care was needed, she massaged horse fat into her scalp at night and washed it out in the morning.

I do agree with her that a shiny nose is not becoming, but until this day, I haven't tried smothering my hair with horse fat overnight. I still wonder: is it really that good for your hair?

Eyebrows

Think of Joan Crawford or Audrey Hepburn. Their eyebrows were part of their signature looks, shaping their faces and giving definition to their eyes and forehead.

Your eyebrows do the same for you and are not to be ignored. Unfortunately, much like the hair on the top of your head, they go white and become invisible. Many older women try to correct this by using a heavy black eyebrow pencil. If it is too black and not applied properly, the dark color gives the face a top-heavy, unnatural appearance. For best results, use an eyebrow pencil in a light brown or gray (not black) tone, and apply it with little feathery, upward strokes. Afterward, brush over them with a toothbrush (again going upward), and erase any strokes that look artificial.

Since my eyebrows are now invisible, I have started to dye them. I do it myself. It is really easy, and the dye is sold in most beauty supply stores. However, I still have them shaped by a girl in my nail salon, and she does a good job. (Most nail salons have professionals who specialize in eyebrows.)

Don't pluck your eyebrows yourself. If you make a mistake, you will not be able to achieve the same shape. It will be a long time before even a professional can correct it.

Eye Shadow

If you use eye shadow at all, a lighter shade works best. Dark shades push your eyes further into your head, something you want to avoid. Most important, avoid sparkling eyes shadows. You don't want your wrinkles to sparkle, and they will if the eye shadow does. Unfortunately, it is not easy to find a good matte eye shadow. When I ask the cosmetic sales girls, they always say, "No, we don't have any matte eye shadow, but so many woman are asking for it."

Maybe if enough women ask for it, they will hear us one day?

Mascara

During an interview on television years ago, the late Estée Lauder once said, "If you don't have enough time for your full makeup routine, apply mascara (always black), and lipstick." She was right; it is more becoming than going without anything.

I apply black mascara to the upper lashes only. Since my lower lashes are a little more sparse now, I make up for it by drawing a thin line with a soft gray pencil along the lower part of my eyes, which gives them more definition.

Avoid waterproof mascara unless you go swimming. It makes lashes stick together, and if you don't separate them right away and the mascara dries, they can look like spider legs—something you want to avoid.

Lipstick

What would you do without lipstick? It is the most important and useful tool in your makeup kit. How often do you say, "I just want to put on some lipstick"? And when you do, it makes you feel so much better instantly. You feel whole again.

Which color should you choose? Don't use dark red or very bright reds. They are harsh, and we need softness now. Stay with lighter shades, or use a lip gloss with color.

I often hear the question, "How can I make my lipstick last?" It is indeed difficult to keep lipstick or lip gloss on for any length of time. Some manufacturers claim that their brand of lipstick stays on for twelve hours, but I have never met a woman who could confirm this. However, there are a few things that can help:

1. **Wipe your lips clean.** This is especially important when reapplying lipstick or gloss during the day.

2. **Lightly powder your lips and the surrounding area.** This will prevent the color from bleeding into the fine lines around your mouth.

3. **Outline the lips with a lip brush or pencil.** A pencil gives a more definite shape. Keep your mouth relaxed and slightly open while tracing the outline, and start from the center, gradually moving to the corners. Use a nude color lip pencil; it will accommodate any color lipstick.

4. **Fill your lips in carefully with lipstick or a brush.** Carry the color far enough inside the mouth so that it looks neat when you talk or smile.

5. **Wait a few minutes for the color to set.** Then, blot your lips with a tissue and reapply your lipstick.

To prevent dryness and chapping, always keep a lip balm handy. If you can't readily reapply your lipstick, you can always pass it discreetly over your lips. Not only does it prevent dryness, but it prevents the lines above the lips from appearing deeper.

Makeup is very individual, and every woman has to experiment to find the right look. But "buyer beware" if you go into a department store and one of the fashionably dressed young women approaches you, smiles, and asks if she can do your makeup. Cosmetics salespeople certainly have a few good tips, but remember: they want you to walk out with as many products as they can talk you into purchasing. No, I am not discouraging you from having a professional makeover, as I am sure you would learn something, but I am advising you to buy only the products you can put on easily by yourself once you are back home.

If a friend tells you about a product that works for her, try it. What do you have to lose? I try everything once, and often I am happy that I did because I learn something.

Tips for Enhancing Your Made-Up Look

- If you wear glasses, put them on when you are ready and check your eye makeup.

- If you put your makeup on in the bathroom or other poorly lit place, go to a window and check yourself out with a hand mirror. You might be surprised to discover that your lipstick is too red, your eye shadow is too strong, or your foundation is too heavy and reveals wrinkles more than necessary.

- Use an eyelash curler before applying mascara; curled eyelashes open up the eye.

- If you use blush, use caution. A little is enhancing, but if your cheeks are really red, blush is aging. We have all seen little old ladies with too much rouge—you must not be one of them! When using powder rouge, apply it with a big brush. Dip it lightly in the rouge and apply on top of your cheekbone, not underneath or it will give you hollow cheeks. But if you don't want to use powder blush, you can get the same effect by putting a dab of your lipstick on your cheekbone and blending it well.

- Keep your makeup looking good throughout the day— a little touch up is needed at least once a day.

- Don't use beauty products you've had for a long time. Yes, makeup has a shelf life too, but since that varies depending on the product, here are some guidelines:

  - Powder: two years

  - Pencil eyeliner: three years

  - Foundation: water-based up to twelve months, oil-based up to eighteen months

  - Lipstick: one to two years, but when it smells rancid, throw it out—it's spoiled

  - Lip liner: up to three years

  - Mascara: four months

- Wash brushes and sponges every week to keep them free of bacteria.

Take Your Face Off

Never, ever, go to bed without taking off your makeup and cleaning your face. There are evenings when I have watched television for too long and all I want to do is fall into my bed. But at the last minute, I pull myself together and wash my face. There are many cleansing and toning products on the market, but who can tell which is the best for you? I can't help you there because I wash my face as I did in the good old days—with water and soap. When it is clean, I splash cold water on it, as cold as my faucets allow, about fifteen times. I am always surprised by the effect; it really stimulates the blood and makes the skin look rosy and fresh.

Giving your face a moisturizing and/or cleaning mask once a week is another way to keep your skin fresh and clean. There are many different choices, and your skin type (dry, normal, or oily) will determine which kind you use. Read the instructions on the package carefully before you buy a product, and if you don't like the feel after using it, try another brand until you see positive results. All beauty products are effective; you just have to find the one that works for you. It really is a matter of trial and error.

I once took part in a *Good Housekeeping* consumer-testing program for a new moisturizing cream. The product contained retinol, and after using it for just a few days, my neck was covered with red bumps and marks. Although I had to go to a dermatologist to have it treated, my girlfriend Gisele swears that creams with retinol have revived her skin. As I said, you never can tell how effective a product will be until you try it.

"Less is more" when we get older, but that doesn't mean wearing no makeup at all.

I see a lot of older women who could take a few years off their faces by wearing a *little* makeup. Please, never say (as I often hear), "I can't be bothered." Please be bothered. You will feel so much better about yourself when you have "put on your face."

CHAPTER 16

Hair:
Your Crowning Glory

*C*alling your hair *your crowning glory* is an expression that has been around for a long time. I did some research to find out where the saying comes from, but didn't have much success. One source suggested that it might come from the mid-to-late 1770s when the French court hairstyles took on extra height, sometimes adding one to one and half times the length of the face. The hair was built up by adding cushions to the head and then covering it with hairpieces. In 1774, the Duchess of Devonshire created a sensation when she introduced ostrich feathers to her hair, which increased the effect of height even more.

But whether the expression dates back to that period cannot be confirmed. Maybe it is much simpler. Perhaps we call it so because it is like a crown on your head and is the first thing people notice about one another. This is a good reason to pay special attention to your hair.

Don't Let Yourself Go

The hundreds of hair products lining the shelves in every

drug store—to thicken, straighten, curl, nourish, condition, revitalize, strengthen, replenish, and reconstruct—should be a great help to you. But looking around, I often wonder if these products deliver what they promise or if some women have not tried any of them. There are a lot of heads out there that would look better with more tender loving care. No, please don't say, "I didn't have time to wash my hair." Of course that can happen, but most of the time it is a question of priorities. Leave the dishes—they will still be there tonight—and wash your hair instead. Walking out of the house looking good is more important, and you will have a better day. Nobody sees the dishes in your kitchen sink, but everybody sees you.

After setting and combing your hair, don't forget to take a hand mirror and look at the back of your head. You might be surprised to see that it doesn't look as good as the front—but it's nothing an extra stroke with a brush or comb can't fix.

A missed or delayed haircut can be a culprit too. Don't let too much time elapse between haircuts. The best way to avoid this is to set up an appointment for your next cut before you leave the salon. You can ask them to confirm your appointment a few days prior, and if you can't go that day, you can always reschedule. That way you won't have to wonder when you need a haircut again. Regular haircuts are good for your hair, which will thank you by truly being your crowning glory!

And speaking of haircuts, the length of your hair makes a big difference. If you don't want to look like an old girl, avoid the over-the-shoulder, down-the-back, loose-hanging styles. If you love your long hair, wear it pulled back in a bun or chignon. These are very becoming looks.

There is no doubt that shorter hairstyles make a woman look younger. We can't hide the extra years with flowing locks; they belong to the young and restless. Of course, how short you wear your hair depends on the type of hair you have. Thick hair can be worn in any style, even very short, because it will always have volume.

I was sitting behind an elderly lady on the bus the other day, and could not take my eyes of her short, bouncy hairstyle. It looked lovely; her thick hair moved with every shake of her head, and I could not help but feel a little envious.

Thinner hair, like mine, needs some length, and in order to get some volume, I have a perm (or a body wave, as it is called now) every three months. You might say, "What! A permanent? No way! My mother had her hair permed, but not me." Yes, our mothers did have curly hair, but a body wave does not necessarily mean curls. If you don't want to look like your mother, you can even wear your hair straight; a body wave will just give it more volume.

Finding a hairdresser who does permanents can be a challenge. A lot of salons that have big signs in the window advertising "cut and blow-dry" usually don't offer them. I once went into a salon where a very young girl greeted me, and when I asked how much they charge for a perm, she looked puzzled and asked, "A what?"

"A permanent," I repeated.

"Let me find out," she said, still not knowing what I wanted. "I'll be right back." With those words, she disappeared for the next ten minutes.

While I waited and looked around, I saw a lot of women with very short skirts that exposed their never-ending legs, who were having young male or female hairdressers coif and dry their hair with huge brushes that pulled their long tresses this way or that.

The young woman finally returned. "I am sorry. We don't do perms anymore," she said, looking at me like I was a relic from another era. I have to admit that at that moment, I was not happy. Did these hip, fashionable hair salons really not want us any more?

But back to the perm: if you consider getting a body wave, check out the hair salons in your neighborhood. They cater to all of us because they are less than "hip". I found my hairdresser in my neighborhood. A friend, my age, had recommended him, and I have been a customer for the last four years.

If you have trouble deciding on the best hairstyle for you, or if you would like a change from the look you have had for years, talk to your hairdresser. To help him understand what you are looking for, show him a picture of a hairstyle you saw in a magazine. It is a starting point, and, knowing your hair, he can tell you what he thinks.

For no other reason than my hair, I would like to be born a man the next time around. Why? Just think about it; there is no setting, no teasing, no straight irons. All a man has to do is wash his hair when he takes a shower, dry it with a towel, and after passing a comb through it— voilá! He is done! And he never gets the comment, "Your hair looks nice *today*." It's the *today* that bothers me and makes me jealous. A man's hair always looks the same, which is not true for women. Only when we have done the washing, setting, and styling does our hair *look nice today*.

And to make matters worse, even when a man doesn't have hair anymore, women will still find him attractive and desirable. How unfair is that?

But since I am a woman, my hair is one of my main challenges. It is fine and not too plentiful, and it doesn't bounce and flow like the hair of the girl on TV who is advertising another miracle product. Some mornings when I get up and look in the mirror, I hope that I don't have to wash it again, and sometimes I don't. I appreciate those mornings when I don't have to fiddle with the rollers and dryer. But a good rule of thumb is that when you ask the question "Do I have to wash my hair?" then yes, it needs a shampoo.

If you have a bald spot (and who doesn't), there is a wonderful product available (online) from Joan Rivers Beauty called Great Hair Day. It is a powder that comes in many shades from blonde to black, and is applied with a brush. It really covers any bald spot, and is especially useful for women who dye their hair black or auburn.

But if you would listen to Mother Nature and allow your hair to stay white, your bold spots wouldn't show. As your hair becomes white and thinner, it blends in with the skin on your skull. To confirm, just look at women with white hair!

What color is your hair? Has the time come when you have to dye it? I remember when I lived in Europe, people were saying that there were no grandmothers in the United States because there were no women with white hair. When I moved here, I found out that there are grand-mothers here, but they hide it well!

When my mother started to dye her hair (she did it her-self), she went through phases of white, blond (light and dark), or orange when something went wrong. Once when her hair was white, we visited a neighbor who had a five-year-old boy, and to his mother's horror he sud-denly asked my mother, "Are you old?"

She wasn't old then, but obviously white hair is a sign of old age, even to a five-year-old.

Thanks to Revlon and L'Oréal, you don't have to look like a grandmother before your time (or ever)!

Hats to the Rescue

If you ever have a bad hair day, or didn't have time to wash your hair, wearing a hat can be the answer.

"I love your hat," I told Marie when we met for lunch.

"Thank you, but I don't look at it as a hat," she answered. "I call it my "cache miser." It is very useful to overcome a bad hair day."

Quoting my grandmother again: "If your hair looks good, and you are wearing nice shoes, the rest will hardly be noticed."

This is true! So try to avoid the bad hair days.

Happy Hair?

Yes, there is such a thing. I recently discovered that when I feel good and happy, my hair does too. It stays in place, has bounce, and shines. You don't have to believe me. Just look at your hair when you feel happy and your world is in place.

When I told my hairdresser about my "happy hair," I expected him to laugh, but quite the contrary: he confirmed it.

"Yes, you are right. When we have customers who are depressed or upset about something, I have the hardest time styling their hair."

Remember that the face is the first thing you see when looking at a person and to enhance it there is nothing better than a nice hairstyle. Neither makeup nor even a beautiful dress can make up for it.

Chapter 17

Happy Hands and Feet

I have to confess that the way my hands have aged upsets me much more than the wrinkles on my face. Maybe it is because I see them all day long? Why are the veins protruding now? They weren't there before. Maybe it is wear and tear? Who knows? But they are permanently there! Drinking water regularly helps minimize their appearance a little, and nail polish helps a lot. No, it doesn't make them disappear, but it diverts the attention.

"I like your nails. Nice color!" I am often told, but I can't take the credit for it because I go every week to have my nails done. I probably could do it myself but a professional manicure is so much better, and the luxury of having it done has made me very lazy. I think I have spent more money on manicures than on any other beauty measure. Fortunately, they are not expensive. I pay fifteen dollars, which includes the tip. But when my budget is tight, I cut out other activities because I feel depressed and unkempt when my nails are not properly maintained.

My color is red—sometimes bright red—and I try to keep them long. But nails don't have to be bright red or long to be beautiful. You might prefer natural colors and shorter nails; what is important is that they are well cared for.

Years ago, when I first started going to a nail salon, I complained to the manicurist about my nails breaking and chipping.

"If you come for a manicure once a week on a regular basis, your nails will grow," she said. She was right. When I miss a week, there is always a nail that breaks or chips.

If your polish starts to come off and is only partially there, either touch it up or take it off. It only takes five minutes, and when somebody looks at them you don't have to pull your hands away, and say, "Oh, I know my nails look terrible, but I didn't have time to do them."

Here are a few, simple steps that will help your nails stay healthy and beautiful and will make your manicure last longer.

1. **Wear rubber gloves when your hands are in water.** This is something we all know, but few of us do!

2. **Open packages with a knife or letter opener, not your nails.** As I struggle to open packaged foods, cleaning products, and many other bags or boxes, I often curse the person who designed them. He or she obviously doesn't have nails, and worse yet, doesn't think of others who have them.

3. **Wear a pair of cotton gloves while vacuuming, dusting, or simply tidying up.** They prevent dirt from getting into your skin and absorb blows to the nails that affect their growth.

4. **Always use hand lotion after washing your hands, and massage cuticles by pushing them back gently.** Vaseline Intensive Care is a good and inexpensive maintenance product.

5. **When away from home, carry an emery board (or nail file) to take care of rough edges immediately.** A very small nick becomes a break when not treated right away.

6. **Keep a top coat handy and apply every other day.** This will make your polish last longer.

The English poet Edith Sitwell used to say, "My hands are my face."

Not being a beautiful woman, she had chosen her hands to speak for her. Luckily, most of us don't have to make that choice, but well-groomed hands always speak well.

Feet

Feet are the stepchildren of the body. You take them for granted until something goes wrong. When bunions or other ailments remind you of how much you need your feet, you pay attention.

But don't wait until trouble reminds you that you have feet: give them some love and care. Please treat yourself to a pedicure at least once a month, and not only in the summer. It's my monthly treat, and I really look forward to having somebody take care of my feet—what a thrill! Adding twenty minutes of leg massage to the experience is totally relaxing and very good for the circulation (and those pesky little veins).

Many salons have specials on Mondays and Tuesdays. Typically, they cost around twenty-nine dollars for both manicure and pedicure, with an extra twelve dollars for the massage. After factoring in the tip, the total price comes to fifty dollars. If you give up one lunch with the girls, you can totally afford it.

And your sandals will also be happy to carry feet that have smooth heels and manicured nails.

Finding the right shoes to avoid putting pressure and stress on your feet is very important. This isn't always easy to do, but following these tips will make finding more comfortable shoes easier:

- Buy your shoes in the afternoon. You will get a better fit than if you buy them in the morning when your feet are still rested.

- Don't let a salesperson tell you that stretching will make the shoe bigger. It rarely helps. They should be comfortable from the minute you put them on; if they aren't, don't buy them.

- Walk around with the shoes in the store. Try to find a spot without carpeting. This is the only way you can tell how the shoes will feel when walking on the street.

- To break in new leather shoes quickly, fill them with lukewarm water. Empty them after after thirty seconds, then wear them until dry. This process will make the shoes more supple and help to adjust to the shape of your foot.

- Wear high heels at home for an hour or two from time to time so you don't lose the ability to walk in them.

CHAPTER 18

Looking Good
Never Goes Out of Style

Ohope my experience as an image consultant will be helpful to you, too. I have worked with many women over the years on improving their wardrobe and image, and as you learned in Chapter 8, I am still doing so today as a volunteer at Bottomless Closet.

Never Give Up on Looking Your Best

While speaking recently to my friend Lydia, who lives in Luxembourg, I asked her how her daughter's mother-in-law, Danny, is doing. (She is the same age as Lydia.)

"Oh, fine," she replied. "She just won't give up. She looks great. Can you imagine, she still wears high-heeled shoes and everything that goes with it!"

What surprised me about her remark was how she clearly understood why Danny looked good: *She hasn't given up.* And that is where the secret lies; you can't give up doing your best when you want to look good. And nothing can help you more than the right clothes. They can hide flaws, and make you look smaller, taller, thinner, and sexier. Most of all, if they are figure-flattering, they can take years off of your appearance!

You might say, "I don't care. I don't dress for others." The reason I strongly disagree with this opinion is that you should not be dressing well for others, but for yourself, because looking good builds your confidence like nothing else will. Just think of the days when you know you look good. Don't you feel more confident? Happier? Doesn't it make your day when somebody says, "You look so nice today," or "What a pretty dress you are wearing"? Isn't this especially true in contrast to the days when you just want to fade into the wall because you didn't care what you put on?

Or you might say, "I want to be comfortable." This too is an excuse for not looking your best. I say excuse because you can be comfortable and still be pretty. Let's look at shoes, for example. Do you really have to wear those clunky, heavy, brown leather sandals? No! There are so many choices of pretty sandals, flats, and medium-heeled shoes available that would make your feet look so much better!

I am not mentioning high heels. I can only say that I am envious, no, extremely jealous, when I see a young girl stride along in three-inch heels—how wonderful! Remembering that once upon a time I also wore three-inch heels does not help. Now, I have a few pairs of high-heeled shoes, ranging from two- to two-and-half inches, but I only wear them when I am going somewhere in a car or when the restaurant is across the street. The one- to one-and-half-inch heels, which I can wear anywhere, anytime, make my feet happy. Thanks to the many attractive choices out there, I can forget about the girl with the three-inch heels.

If a pair of shoes with a one- to one-and-a-half-inch heel is uncomfortable, try shoes with a wedge heel—the extra support makes the difference and will allow you to still wear a shoe with a heel.

However, "looking good" does not happen by itself. It takes a little time. It always did, but now that we are older, it takes even longer. A few weeks ago, Gisele stayed over, and in the morning, after being in the bathroom for some time, she came out and said, "Isn't it amazing how much longer it takes now to get ready?"

I had to agree. But besides needing more time, you need a commitment to yourself not to be lazy or negligent, but to take the extra time to get ready!

Without over-emphasizing the importance of appearance, don't forget that the biggest asset you have in life is *you*, and when it comes to clothes, you are the product and your clothes are the wrapping. Voltaire, the eighteenth-century French philosopher, once said, "Dress changes the manner." This was true in the eighteenth century, and is still true today.

Looking good is the best way to make you feel good. It lifts your spirits, and makes you forget about your age.

I once heard the American designer Halston tell an interviewer on television, "People who can't get it together are uninterested in themselves and lack self-respect."

The best proof of how good you look is when other women look at you! Pay attention on the days you feel pretty and good about yourself, and you will see how many envious glances you get from other women.

Allow me to digress for a moment, as I must tell you that I have always been glad that humans wear clothes. Not only because they keep us warm in the winter, but because they protect us from being naked. You can imagine it wouldn't be pretty if everybody was like the emperor in the story "The Emperor's New Clothes." Maybe it was the graphic, ugly illustrations of him without clothes that had first impressed this idea upon me when I was a child.

When the bloom of youth dies, most women have a little of this or that they would rather not show, and that is why the habit of adorning your body with clothes and jewelry is such a blessing!

CHAPTER 19

The Influence of Designers and the Help of Fashion Magazines

Today the names of designers are as familiar to us as the brands of cereal on the supermarket shelves. Even if we don't wear Gucci or Chanel, we know who they are. Besides their fame for creating beautiful clothes, they have achieved a near rock-star status through their personalities, their much publicized lifestyles, and often their signature looks (for example, Karl Lagerfeld always dresses in a black suit, white shirt, dark glasses, and his hair in a ponytail), all resulting in a notoriety that gives women a form of security and reassurance.

It would be hard for us to imagine a world without designers. But how did it all start?

Haute Couture

The term *haute couture*, French for creating exclusive and often trend setting fashions, might lead you to believe that designer fashions started in France. But not so! It was started by an Englishman by the name of Charles Frederick Worth.

At the age of twelve, Worth became an apprentice in the famous London drapery store Swan & Edgar. Working there for the next eight years, and observing the *beau monde* (beautiful people), he learned about fabrics and style. Having noticed that all new ideas came from Paris, he moved there when he was twenty.

He found employment with the fashionable store Gagelin-Opigez & Cie. When Marie Vernet, one of the sales girls (whom he had married), wore dresses in the store that he had designed, clients started to ask who had made them. With his reputation growing, he opened his own store at 7 rue de la Paix (today one of Paris's most elegant shopping avenues). Until then, royalty, the nobility, and the rich were dressed by seamstresses, who were not known for their innovative styles. But Charles Worth changed all that: for the next five decades he dressed the most powerful and prosperous women of Europe.

Since Charles Frederick Worth brought *haute couture* to life more than 150 years ago, many gifted men and women have followed him, keeping our love and fascination with designers alive.

Fashion Magazines

Reading fashion magazines like *Vogue* and *Harper's Bazaar* is the best and simplest way to stay abreast of what is "in" or "out" of style. However, many women never buy them because they can't identify with what they see. Yes, the clothes are expensive, and the models are unreal. But if you can put that aside, knowing what to look for and how to interpret what you see will help you plan a wardrobe for the upcoming season and show you how to update what you already own.

Here are a few tips to help you:

1. **Don't be intimidated.** It is indeed unsettling to see women, clothes, and situations that are so far removed from your surroundings and lifestyle. How can anyone compete with that gorgeous creature looking out at you? How can anyone afford to pay those prices, and how could anyone possibly leave her blouse open as far as the model does in the picture?

2. **Learn by analyzing.** Study the makeup, hairstyles, and clothing. Study how they are worn and how they are accessorized. If not everything is suitable for you, you might find out that some of the jewelry looks like what you have laying in the back of your drawers. Seeing it on the pages of *Vogue,* you know that it can come out and you can wear it again.

3. **Study the new silhouettes.** Become familiar with the popular shapes and forms of a season's look. When looking at a particular piece of clothing, consider these questions before making decisions about clothes you already own (or want to buy):

   - Is it for full or slim-figured women?
   - Is it long or short?
   - Is the waist marked, or do loose shapes predominate?
   - Is it feminine or tailored?

4. **Consider the colors.** Although burgundy might be the color of the season, there are many other colors that complement it. The color singled out as the latest fashion is not the only color, but the dominant one. If your wardrobe does not include burgundy, think about adding a piece of clothing—a pair of shoes, a scarf, or a handbag—the choice is yours.

5. **Assess how the clothing is worn.** If you are wondering why your raincoat does not look as good as the one in the magazine, let me reassure you that the difference is not only in the model wearing it. Look again at the picture: the collar is turned up and the sleeves are turned back. Instead of being buttoned up to the neck, two or three buttons are left open for a casual and relaxed look. The belt is pulled in, with the material evenly adjusted. This observation can be made for all the garments you see in *Vogue*, and adopting it is an easy way to look smarter without spending a penny.

6. **Modify a high-fashion hairstyle.** Much like the clothes in the magazine, the featured hairstyles are exaggerated versions of the latest trend, and not necessarily how you would wear your own hair in daily life. However, seeing faces framed by a halo of curls confirms that curls are in style, and you should try to adapt a curlier version of your current hairstyle accordingly. You may wish to experiment with short curls, shoulder-length curls, or just curls at the ends. Whatever you choose is up to you, but the message is clear—straight is out!

7. **Pay attention to accessories.** They are an excellent way to update your look and complete an outfit. They can also make a statement about a woman's personality or become a personal insignia.

Accessories

Jewelry caters to a woman's greatest weakness: her vanity. This is why, going far back into the history of any civilization, jewelry has always been associated with being feminine. But much like clothing, jewelry has to be tried on before purchasing. A pretty, small pendant can look very attractive lying on the counter, but it could disappear on a larger woman.

To use jewelry effectively, avoid anything that looks ordinary. This applies as much to size as design. If you want a pair of button earrings, don't settle for a pinhead size; they should be visible. Don't buy dull gold, as it will give the impression that you are trying not to be there. Shiny, bright gold jewelry will light up your face. Mediocre jewelry doesn't look exciting and could say the wrong thing about its wearer.

Scarves have become a major accessory over the last few years. Some women love to wear scarves and arrange them well. Others struggle to keep them in place, trying to prevent them from slipping and sliding all day long. Don't blame yourself for an unruly scarf! If it's made of a synthetic or slippery fabric, like acetate or a heavy silk, you will have trouble keeping it in place. To wear a scarf with ease, choose an oblong style in a soft silk or chiffon.

The magazines will show you how this season's scarves are worn.

If you can't find an attractive chiffon scarf, or the color you want is not available, buy a yard of fabric. Don't worry about hemming it. The sides are selvage and need no attention. On the ends, all you have to do is pull some threads until you have a small fringe.

Handbags are often referred to as a status symbol. They communicate taste, money, class, elegance, and youthfulness. Bags, like scarves, have become an important accessory over the last few years. And even if you use the same bag every day, and you have lots of other bags sitting in the closet at home, don't you have trouble resisting those beautiful new styles that are tempting you everywhere? Many bags have convenient shoulder straps, but if your bag is too heavy, it can hurt your shoulders over time and eventually make you hunch over.

Lighten your bag by going through it from time to time and taking out what you have forgotten was in there!

Shoes rival handbags when it comes to status symbols. The late Coco Chanel said, "A woman with a good pair of shoes is never ugly."

Very true. A good, expensive pair of shoes can save any outfit. (Remember the saying, if your hair looks good and you are wearing nice shoes, the rest will hardly be noticed?) What *will* be noticed is when your shoes are outdated. If you are like most of us, you have accumulated a lot of shoes over the years. These include shoes with heels that are too high and hurt your feet, those you don't have an occasion for, and those that fit properly in the store but never afterward. Seeing all those shoes at the bottom of your closet, you might hesitate to buy new ones and always wear your comfortable loafers. But are your loafers even the latest style? (Yes, they change style, too.) This is also true for sneakers—with their different colors and the variety of materials used today, they have become a fashion item. You should draw inspiration from the models in the magazines when you go to replace your old shoes.

Sunglasses add instant sex appeal and mystery (and we can still use some of that) to a woman's look by hiding her eyes, in addition to fulfilling their original purpose of protecting the eyes from sun and glare.

It is necessary to buy a new pair at least every two years. Please avoid cheap ones, such as those sold for a few dollars on the street. Sunglasses have become an important fashion accessory, and like jewelry, they should be shiny and sparkly statement pieces. When they lack a refined style and finish, they don't stand up to daily wear and tear, which makes the lenses more likely to become scratched, and dull lenses detract from their appeal.

To restore a shiny look to sunglasses, make a paste with talcum powder (baby powder) and water. Rub the glasses well with this paste. After rinsing and polishing, your glasses will look like new.

If you don't have a subscription to a fashion magazine—maybe you could ask for one as a birthday present from your children one year—at least buy one from time to time. It will give you an idea what fashion is all about today, and if you keep your eyes open, you'll be pleased to discover how up-to-date some of the items in your wardrobe are again.

CHAPTER 20

Choosing Your Most Flattering Styles

Never has the choice of clothing been greater, and never before has getting dressed been done more haphazardly than today. Maybe the many choices are confusing, or maybe it is because there are no more rules—everything goes, at any time, anywhere.

But not for you. You need to be well-groomed and wear clothes that are becoming and appropriate for your age and lifestyle.

Dress for Success . . . and Your Age

Years ago when my mother and I owned a boutique in New York, a lady in her seventies who had little gray curls came in and asked the price of a white, frilly cotton dress with a transparent lacy top that was displayed in the window. My mother told her the price, and added, "I am sure your granddaughter will look very pretty in that dress."

"It's not for my granddaughter, it's for me," the woman hissed. Needless to say, there was no sale.

A more realistic approach came from Elli, my friend in Switzerland who is eighty-six years old. I had sent a Ralph Lauren scarf that was part of his latest collection. When she telephoned to thank me, she said, "I have just seen a fashion show from New York on television and loved the tight black pants and colorful tops worn with the flowing scarves. If I was younger, I would have bought the whole outfit, but since it would not be appropriate for me anymore, the scarf you sent helps me to feel a little up-to-date, too. Thank you again."

Dos and Don'ts

I am an optimist, but I am also a realist, and I have to agree with the designer Karl Lagerfeld, who said, "Nothing makes you look older than trying to look young."

So before we look at what is appropriate and becoming, let us first identify what is not.

Regrettably, there are things that belong to *long ago*. Until the day she died, my mother resisted new fashions and struggled with being too attached to the styles of a bygone day. Whenever we went shopping, or she looked at *Vogue* or catalogues, she would say, "I wonder who they make these clothes for. Who can wear these things?"

Not wanting to hurt her feelings, I would answer hesitantly, "They are made for younger women!"

"Do they really think everybody is young?" she replied, wearing a look of disbelief.

No, they don't. The designers and clothing manufacturers know that most of the female population today is still under the age of sixty-five, but may it be said that that is changing with every day as more baby boomers join the ranks of senior citizens.

"They're baby boomers—like, you know, really old."

Fashion Don'ts for the Mature Woman

Please don't feel deprived by these *don'ts*. Embracing them will make you like yourself better when you look in the mirror.

Too many layers: Don't bury yourself under layers and layers of fabric. I have a friend who most of the time wears a camisole, a blouse, a cardigan, a coat, and a big shawl draped over all of it. Even in the summer, she finds ways to put layer over layer. Yes, layering has become popular, but it should not hide the person and conceal a nice figure, which this friend of mine still has.

Shorts: Naturally, shorts are cooler in the summer, but doesn't your vanity compel you to hide marks and veins? And even if you don't have veins, your legs are not what they used to be. Whenever I see an elderly woman in shorts, I think, *Would long pants really have been so much more uncomfortable?* In warmer weather, a long flowing skirt or capris could be an option to feel cool and look good!

Camisoles: These tiny tops are for young women who don't need a bra. Bra straps are not attractive, and neither is a little extra flesh under the arms. However, if you wear a shirt or a top with a deep neckline over it, a camisole is still an option.

Flip-flops: Worn by men, women, and children everywhere and for every occasion, flip-flops seem to be the holy grail of shoes and an answer to all prayers. Although they began as beachwear, they are now worn all over the world—and nobody is listening to the warnings from doctors that they are harmful for your feet and legs. Avoid flip-flops by replacing them with a nice pair of low-heeled sandals.

Short skirts: Even on a pair of good legs, super-short miniskirts are not flattering anymore because they give off a message of youth, which the rest of your body and face will contradict.

Short sleeves: Elbows are not the most attractive part of your body at any age, but as you get older, you should look for styles that are most flattering for your arms and avoid styles that finish just above the elbow. Sometimes sleeves that are halfway down your arm are best, and sometimes styles with very short sleeves look better. You have to negotiate this by examining your arms and seeing what is most flattering to you.

Tight clothing: Some people believe wearing tight clothing makes them look slimmer, but just the opposite is true. Looking like you have been poured into a pair of pants or a top points out every little extra ounce of fat. Strive instead for a style that is a little loose, not baggy or tent-like—just loose, which is more becoming.

Tight waistbands: If the waistband of your pants or skirt is too tight, it will push up the flesh. Even if you don't have a spare tire, a too-tight waistband will give you one. This applies to underwear as well. Make sure the elastic of your panties is not too tight around your waist or the top of your legs. They should not be so snug as to create little muffin tops.

Bikinis: Please don't laugh, but I have seen plenty of older women who sun themselves in—yes—a bikini. As this style doesn't support anything—least of all the stomach—it is not a pretty sight.

Jeans with holes: While showing off young skin with a pair of ripped jeans might be sexy, a more mature woman with holes in her pants looks like she wants to compete with her granddaughter.

Large floral or geometric prints: These patterns over-power the wearer. Instead of the person wearing the dress, the dress will be wearing the person. By large flowers, I mean the size of a sunflower or cabbage rose.

Crewnecks: The cut finishes just at the base of the neck, which emphasizes your neck. You can agree this is some-thing to avoid because you don't want to attract the atten-tion to your neck, right?

Old bras: You know those bras you have had for years that don't pinch and pull anywhere, and which are soooo comfortable? The ones you wear around the house? Well, they have to go. Why? Look at where your bust is—not in the right place, which is something easily corrected with a new bra!

By the way, if you are ever tempted to go braless—oh, yes, it feels so good—don't succumb, because that weak-ens the support muscles even more.

Very long, dangling earrings: I can't really say why, but they just don't look right anymore. Maybe they are like a very short skirt, pointing out that we are not so young anymore.

Smart Choices for Mature Women

Before going into specifics, I have to ask you an important question: Do you have a full-length mirror?

When I worked with clients in their homes and asked that question, half of them answered, "I don't have one. I just go into the bathroom and look."

"In the bathroom? You see yourself only to the waist or a little below. You can't see if your skirt or pants are the right length, or if your shoes match the rest of your outfit."

One client responded, "Yes, I do. It's behind the door there. I have trouble getting to it because there is so much junk in front of it."

If you don't have one, or you can't get to it, I implore you to correct this situation immediately. And please hang it in a place where you can check yourself out at a glance. Remember, just as with a magnifying mirror for your makeup, you don't know how you look unless you see yourself!

Now that you know what is unbecoming, and you have a mirror in place, we can focus on what is flattering.

Lighter colors: If you wear a lot of black, mix it with white, yellow, pink, light blue, and light gray. These colors can be worn in pastel shades or brighter tones. They are more flattering to the skin. And if you find black too harsh and want to get away from it, navy blue is an alternative. It is still dark, but not as intense.

Dark colors: These are good for places where you pack on the extra pounds, like your hips and thighs. When you are tired, it is best not to wear black or other dark colors next to your face. Wear a light color that will lift you up!

Show off your curves: If you have a bigger bust (some women would give their right arm for one), don't hide it under layers of clothes: this makes you look like a tent. Instead, wear styles that hug the body at the waist, such as a wrap dress or a shirtmaker style. What's a shirt-maker? You know the style that has been around since the 1950s. It has a button-down front and is belted, with either a full or straight skirt. It's a fashionable and flattering look.

If your waist is still one of your assets, tuck your blouse into your jeans, pants, or skirt. This conveys a younger image than wearing a loosely hanging top. And always wear a belt with jeans when the waistband shows. This finishes the look with a youthful touch.

Necklines: Feel free to experiment with a variety of necklines: scoop neck, v-neck, a loose cowl, or a boat neckline. They all show some skin—or your *décolleté* (cleavage)—which is something we can still show for many years to come. Just be careful how *much* cleavage you show: a teaser is better than too much.

Prints: Both small and large scattered prints in pastel colors can be very flattering and feminine. Stay away from the small, tight, floral prints that recall your grandmother's aprons. And remember that large, bright prints overpower the wearer. If you are a lover of patterns, wear them as part of an outfit; for example, patterned pants and a solid top, or a floral top with solid pants or a skirt. This is a very becoming look for heavier women too.

Zippers, buttons, collars, and pockets: All these extras give a garment a "snappy" image. Zippers can be left open to wherever it is suitable or desirable. This is also true for buttons. Collars can be turned up, and lots of pockets give you a casual, younger image.

Safari styles: These styles, à la Ralph Lauren, are sporty and youthful, yet at the same time are conservative and always appropriate. When wearing a shirt or jacket, always turn up the sleeves and wear the collar up.

Sleeveless vests: Vests are very useful for hiding your love handles and spare tires while projecting a youthful look. They are suitable over a shirt or dress for summer, and over a sweater for winter.

Sweater sets: If sweaters hug you tighter than you would like, wearing a matching cardigan over it is a smart choice for achieving camouflaging comfort.

Well-fitting bras: You need bras that support, lift, and separate the breasts. These are not easy to find, especially in department stores where there are hundreds of different styles and brands competing for your attention and no salespeople to assist you. But specialty stores with trained staff to help you will measure you and find the best form for your bust.

If you need a minimizer to make your breasts look smaller, be careful that it does not flatten the breast, leaving you shapeless.

Raincoat: This useful garment has become a fashion item over the years, replacing the spring and fall coats that were fashionable long ago. As it is a fashion item, replace it at least every two years. The trench coat is the most becoming style—at any age—because of its attractive details, such as epaulets, pockets, and belt. Yes, it's a classic style, so you might ask, "Why do I have to replace it?" Well, a few years of wear and tear does not improve a garment's freshness. Finding another trench coat made with a different fabric and color will update your look.

Red shoes: No girl should be without a pair of red shoes. Since shoes and handbags don't have to match any longer, red shoes will complement 90 percent of what you have in your wardrobe. They really uplift a simple black dress, or pants and a sweater. No matter the style, they give *pizzazz* to your image.

Red shoes have always had a little magic—think of the Hans Christian Anderson story *The Red Shoes*, or of the red shoes that carried Dorothy home in *The Wizard of Oz*. If you think red shoes are only for the young, look at Pope Benedict XVI who, in his eighties, is still wearing red shoes.

Whether we realize it or not, or we think it is important or not, we are all deeply influenced by how somebody looks. Remember that making a good first impression is important—this old adage is still as true as ever! You will never forget how a person looked when you first met them.

CHAPTER 21

Let Go of the Clothes You Don't Wear Anymore

Now that you know what is becoming and what is not, you must be ready to go shopping.

Not so fast! First we need to make room in your closet. We have to get rid of the cobwebs, the memories from long ago, and the clothes that belonged to a body you don't have anymore.

Yes, they are all there! Keeping clothes you don't wear anymore and seeing them hang in your closet can make you feel sad and nostalgic. They can even bring back memories that tug at your heart.

"That's the dress I wore when John and I first dated," Patricia told me, holding up a pretty, red cocktail dress.

Patricia will never forget John, and she doesn't need the red dress to remember him by, but seeing it again and again was like pushing the arrow into to her heart a little deeper.

Or do you want to be reminded by that slinky, short summer dress that you are not a size eight anymore? That was another time, another life! Keeping that dress will never bring that time back, but it will be a constant reminder that you aren't that person or that size any longer.

Wall-to-wall clothing, but nothing to wear is a cliché we have all heard. It makes us smile every time because we have to admit, *That's me.*

There are two reasons why that *is* you, and why you don't have anything to wear. First: *there are too many items in your wardrobe,* making it impossible to know what you have. How can you choose from a rack that is tightly packed with items you can't really see? So you are most likely wearing a few things again and again and ignoring the rest.

The second reason: *you have trouble giving things away.*

"Oh no, I paid a lot of money for that coat," Irene told me.

"When did you wear it last?" I asked her.

"Can't remember, it must be years ago!"

The coat was bulky and took up a lot of room, and just because it was expensive was no reason to hang onto it when Irene didn't wear it anymore.

And then there is the *in case*—in case you lose weight (which most of the time doesn't happen) or in case you have to go to party. Do you really think the dress from ten years ago will do you justice in the event there is a party? No, not everything comes back. The look might, but it always has a little, different twist. Furthermore, the fabric of garments hanging in the closet for a long time can look pretty tired.

And a third reason, if you need another one, is that for most of us who are retired or semiretired, the kind of clothes we now wear is very different from the ones we needed when going to work every day.

Some days when you open your closet, can't you hear your business suits and work clothes ask you, "What are you going to do with us? What did we do wrong? You haven't worn us in a long time." They feel neglected. The best way to bring them back to life is to donate them to an organization that recycles them (like Bottomless Closet or Dress for Success), which helps women join the workforce, and they can look the part wearing your suit.

I love my friend Peggy Anne's philosophy. When she doesn't wear something anymore, she says, "Let somebody else enjoy it."

Taking Charge of Your Closet

Cleaning out your closet is a major event. It takes time, so set aside a day or two, and if you have a girlfriend whose taste you trust, ask for her help. Another option is to hire a wardrobe consultant.

I say it is a major event because you literally have to look at each piece of clothing hanging in your closet and make a decision about it, and then answer questions like,

- Does it still suit me?

- Do I still like it?

- Does it still fit me?

- Do I still need it?

And when in doubt, you have to try it on—a nuisance, I know, but that is the only way to get your answer. If the item is a reject, fold it immediately and put it in the bag you have prepared for donations. Why do I mention this? Because I have seen too many women put an item to the side but have second thoughts when they see it later, and they put it back in the closet.

When your task is done and you are looking with great relief at your pared-down wardrobe and all those empty hangers, you will agree that *less is more.*

Knowing what to wear will be so much easier.

And needing less brings with it another advantage: you can buy a more expansive variety of clothing. When you went to work every day and had to dress differently all the time, your budget was stretched to get the most for the money. Now, instead of buying items on sale or trying to find three tops for the price of one, a fancy blouse you have seen in a boutique can be yours.

Let's go back for a moment to those of you who are having trouble giving things away. Do you have a granddaughter? That might change things a little.

Did you have a grandmother? Well, then you will remember how excited you were when she allowed you to go through her closets and look in her drawers—and it will be the same for your granddaughter.

If you have clothes that are a reflection of a time gone by—like my blue jeans from the seventies painted all over with faces and stars, or you have a leather skirt with fringes, or a sequined bolero, or a fur stole you haven't worn in years but always kept—your granddaughter could be the answer.

In one of my closets, I have reserved a spot where I keep what I call Cosette's clothes. When I showed them to her and told her they were hers, she said, "But Moma, they are too big for me. Maybe they'd fit Mami?"

"They would, darling, but I don't think Mami would wear them."

And then I went on to explain, "When you become a teenager, you will have a lot of fun with your friends looking at these. And your friends will laugh and say, 'What? Your grandmother wore those jeans?'"

Not quite understanding what I was talking about, she touched an embroidered peasant dress and asked, "Is that mine, too?"

"Yes, it is."

And while passing her little fingers over the embroidery she said: "I like this one a lot."

I am looking forward to seeing her wear that dress one day. But if I don't, the thought that she might wear it gives it a whole new meaning! (All that costume jewelry you are not wearing anymore can have the same purpose: it will delight your granddaughter and remind her of you!)

If I have still not convinced you to pare down your wardrobe, let me remind you that everything you don't wear anymore could be a great help for a person in need.

There are many organizations to donate to, and some

even come and pick up. Check out your local neighborhood, your church, or check on line for nonprofit organizations. They will all appreciate your generosity, and you will know that your "good red coat" is once more fulfilling its purpose.

CHAPTER 22

The Joys of Shopping

Shopping—a magical word—is one of life's great pleasures for women. You go shopping to buy new clothes, entertain yourself, meet your girlfriends, and you even go shopping to chase away the blues.

The bags dangling on your arms when you walk out of a store make you feel victorious. You have a new dress, a new top, new shoes, or maybe just new cosmetics or pantyhose, but whatever it is, it makes you feel good, renewed.

I am always impatient to get home and look at my newfound treasure again, and when I hang it in my closet, everything else takes a backstage.

But to combine this pleasure with good results is a challenge. There are many pitfalls; the most dangerous are sales and impulse buying, which are actually one and the same. There is hardly a woman (including me) who can resist a huge sale sign.

"Oh, let's go in and see what there is!" my girlfriend says, and we step in.

There are many temptations, like price tickets where a red marker has overridden the price of $69.95 to make it

$29.95. Wow! What a deal, and regardless of need, appropriateness, or the fact that you have similar items hanging in your wardrobe, the $29.95 top has a new home.

I love sales, too, but I learned my lesson when, after making some impulsive purchases during a sale, I had no budget for the winter coat I badly needed.

By the way, if there were only men in the world, sales would not be a great success. Being in the fashion business, I often had the opportunity to go to sample sales of companies like Burberry and Perry Ellis. When the sale started at 10:00 a.m., and I arrived at 10:30 a.m., women were already heading to the elevator with bags and bags of merchandise and making it difficult to get out of the elevator.

On the other hand, the few men who were there went to the cash register holding two shirts, a tie, and a few pairs of socks—even Burberry's greatly reduced prices didn't make them indulge. Men only buy what they need, and not because it is a deal.

Sometimes, I would tell Marc, "You know, there is a sample sale this week at Perry Ellis. What do you want?"

"Nothing, really."

"Really? But they have nice things for men, and the prices are so much better than in a store."

"Yes, but I don't need anything!"

How can men not need anything? Why is that? Maybe because men can wear the same blue suit to work for a week and nobody notices or would dare make a remark.

If a woman wore the same yellow dress twice in a week, her colleagues would say, "Did you see? She is wearing that dress again. I wonder if she has anything else?"

But I am so glad that, as a woman, I can count shopping as one of my pleasures in life.

Preparing for Your Shopping Excursion

Now that you've cleaned out your wardrobe, you have an idea of what to add and what you need for the new season. However, it might be a good idea to make a list, just as you would for the supermarket, because it is so easy to forget when your best intentions are overruled by a huge price reduction. Furthermore, by consulting your list, you will refrain from buying that adorable sweater that won't go with anything else you own.

Here are a few more tips for avoiding mistakes in your wardrobe:

- **Make sure you need something before you buy it.**

- **Don't buy something if you don't or won't have an occasion to wear it.**

- **Don't buy anything without trying it on.** There may be a long line for the fitting room, but if the article is on sale, remember it is not returnable.

- **Ignore the size label.** If something fits you, it's your size. If the tag says size 14 and you think you are a size 12, don't worry: you didn't put on weight. Every clothing manufacturer today has its own measurements.

- **Never buy a garment that is a little tight.** You might think that you will lose weight in the near future, but remember how many times you didn't? Seeing this top or dress will frustrate you every time you see it hanging in your closet. First, it will remind you that you haven't lost the weight. Second, you will experience the displeasure of having spent money for a dress you can't wear. Even a tiny woman looks fat in a tight garment. Better to buy things a bit larger because you will look slimmer in a slightly looser outfit.

- **Don't judge a garment by how it looks on the hanger.** The look of a garment on a hanger should not influence you. It might look drab hanging there, but stunning on you. Or it might be beautiful on the hanger, but not on you. Always try something on before making a decision.

- **Check out the fit of a garment.** Make sure you can see yourself from the back and from the side. (If the store doesn't have a three-way mirror, use your mirror from your makeup kit in your handbag.) Make sure the garment does not pull or pucker in the wrong places.

  - *Shoulder seams:* Unless the style demands otherwise, the shoulder seam should be on your natural shoulder line. If the seams are in too far, the garment will look too small; seams hanging over the shoulders will make it look too big.

  - *Pants:* When you stand straight, pants should not pull in the crotch area or pucker in the back. In length, they should cover your heel half way. If they are longer, they can easily be shortened, but when they are too short, letting out a hem often leaves a mark that does not totally disappear with dry cleaning or pressing.

- *Blouses and jackets:* When blouses or jackets pull across the front and gape when buttoned, they are too small.

● **Buy a whole outfit or separates that match.** Avoid buying just a skirt or only a top. Designers take great care to create clothes that match, but since each piece is sold individually now, we often make the mistake of buying only one piece or the other, making it difficult later to find a perfect match.

● **Take along anything you are trying to match.** When you are trying to match a garment in your wardrobe take it with you when you go shopping to be sure the pieces will go together. After all, it is difficult to know if a particular tone of beige will match your jacket unless you see the pieces together.

● **Don't get blinded by the 50 percent discount.** There are stores who have merchandise specially made for their sales, so that price "reduction" might be off the manufacturer's suggested value. Not all sales are created equal.

● **Stay loyal to a brand.** If a certain manufacturer's style and cut fit you well and you like their designs, stay with them. The grass is not always greener on the other side, but you may think so because the exhaustive selections and sale offers everywhere make you forget.

- **Consider how you feel in a garment.** When you slip into a dress, a coat, or a suit, it should instantly make you feel better. If you think it looks nice but you don't feel quite right in it, it's not for you. Don't convince yourself that it's not bad. Not bad is not good enough. Remember, if you feel good in your clothes, you will move well in them. You will project assurance and confidence. Therefore, whenever you hesitate or are in doubt, don't buy it. You should love something the minute you put it on.

And the last tip, which I know from experience to be true:

- **Trust your own judgment.** You know what looks best on you. Many women say, "But I don't know what suits me." Yes, you do. Just take a moment to look at yourself and ask, "Do I like this? Does it make me look good? Does it feel comfortable?" Be careful when taking a friend's advice. She is not in your skin, and her approval shouldn't make you buy a garment you don't feel comfortable in. I know you have the answer. Just look again.

If you are worried that all these *dos and don'ts* are a lot of tiring work, I have to agree it looks that way. But once you get into the habit of shopping with these tips in mind, it becomes second nature. Don't overlook your silver lining here. You now have the luxury of taking your time and paying more attention to yourself, which you weren't able to do for years. So take it slow and enjoy the ride to becoming comfortable and well-dressed in clothes that make you look your best.

Undergarments Count!

Now that you look good on the outside, what about underneath? I mean your underwear! What do you mean nobody sees it? Aren't *you* somebody? Remember the feeling when you wore silky underpants and lacy bras? Remember how feminine and sexy it felt?

Speaking for myself, nice underwear always makes me feel more feminine, more desirable.

Liking nice underwear must be another characteristic of my family. My grandmother Katherine's motto was "One always has to be dressed to make love or to go to the hospital."

She held doctors in high esteem, and making a good impression was important to her—as was making love—well, I can only assume that she knew all about it!

She had two husbands and at least one lover. Her first husband (with whom she had two daughters) divorced her after finding her with another man when he returned from the war. She lived in sin (as it was called then) with the second man in her life, who was my mother's father, because his wife wouldn't give him a divorce.

Later in life, she met my grandfather William. He was a war veteran, and when he received a government pension and compensation for being buried alive during World War I, she married him. The pension didn't hurt, but he also fulfilled another belief of hers: "To have a good marriage, the man has to love the woman a little more than she loves him."

Even when William didn't agree with her, he always indulged her with an affectionate smile and said, "Ja, ja, just go ahead. I know you will do it your way anyway."

Whether you want to impress the doctor or who knows whom else you might meet, pass through the lingerie department before leaving the store just to see what is there. You might be surprised by the new fabrics underwear is made of today. They are very smooth and comfortable, often doing away with seams and giving more support. All of these modifications are meant to make your clothes fit better.

Going shopping and finding *exactly* what you want takes time. From my own experience, I know how overwhelming it is in department stores when floor after floor is filled with hundreds of the same item. Who has so much time (and energy) to work through floor after floor to find the right thing? Yet there is a better way. Start buying in boutiques or specialty stores where you won't be confused by the amount of merchandise, and . . . you will get personal attention!

CHAPTER 23

A Smile Changes Everything

Asmiling face is a pretty face at any age. Being friendly can get you anything. Most elderly people are friendly and polite, but some are not, like the lady in the supermarket the other day. She was very displeased that there was no shopping cart available, and when I got one for her, there was no thank-you. She was just as unhappy with the shopping cart as she had been without it.

Others leave their shopping carts in the middle of an aisle with no regard for who would like to pass by. I have always wondered why seniors go shopping at the same time as working folks. Wouldn't it be easier to go when the stores are empty and there is no struggle to get to the shelves?

The mother of Wendy, who was a client of mine for many years before we became friends, was a very difficult, demanding lady, and she did not make Wendy's life easy. One day when Wendy was struggling unsuccessfully—again—to please her mother, she got angry and said, "Mother, I know you are mad and unhappy, but it is not my fault that you're old."

Getting older is nobody's fault; it is life's way of making room for the young. As an older person myself, many times I have seen how young people are happy to help a smiling, friendly senior, yet turn away from a grouchy, sad-looking, demanding person who shows little regard for the surrounding world.

It is indeed hard to resist somebody with a warm, engaging smile, someone who listens and is interested in what is going on, and who can voice his or her opinions in a pleasant, nonconfrontational way. A smile on your face will attract people to you, and you will be an inspiration to them. Also, cracking a joke about yourself breaks the ice.

"Haven't you heard the bell?" my son asks when I don't get to the door fast enough.

Instead of being irritated by his tone, I say, "You know I am a little deaf and slow now, give me a break!"

It makes him laugh, and I get a hug when he passes me.

Going into Zara, a fashionable boutique on Fifth Avenue, I asked a young sales man (whose attention I only got after he had finished chatting with his very attractive, not-more-than-twenty-years-old colleague), "Do you have warm-up suits?"

He looked at me in disbelief.

"What are you looking for?" he asked.

After a moment, he continued.

"Oh, no, we don't carry those things."

Hearing him refer to warm-up suits as *those things,* I realized my mistake. Years ago I would have been offended by the young man's attitude and his condescending tone of voice, but not anymore. As I walked out of the store, I smiled to myself, thinking *You should have known better—what were you thinking?"* I wasn't. I didn't consider that a chic boutique on Fifth Avenue wouldn't be selling clothes for old ladies to be comfortable in. It was my mistake.

Yes, the young man could have been a little more indulgent, but by not blaming him, the blunder didn't spoil my day. Instead, it made me laugh at myself.

Humor is the best defense in life. Seeing the funny side changes everything for the better. And while you are smiling, remember that using your charm can get you what you want, and if you can add some kindness with it, you will make the world a better place and at the same time feel better about yourself.

Unfortunately, charm was not something my mother had in abundance. She was very amusing and a good storyteller, and she made people laugh, but her judgmental behavior and lack of patience caused her a lot of grief. She never hesitated to voice her opinion about somebody's behavior or work.

My grandmother, on the other hand, was a gentle woman. When she did not agree or understand what somebody did, she would shrug her shoulders and say, "Our Lord has many different animals in his kingdom."

She was well liked, and with her down-to-earth approach to life, she was always ready to lend a helping hand, as she did when Jacques and I arrived in Germany during a bitterly cold January. We had come to stay for a year, which meant we needed to find work.

After reading the want ads every day, Jacques went to many interviews with little success, and every evening we hoped that the next day would be a better one. One evening after dinner, my grandmother got up from the table and went into the bedroom. When she came back, she had 100 Deutsche mark note in her hand. She put it on the table in front of Jacques and said, "Here is a DM 100. Tomorrow I want you to go and buy a decent coat. In that poor looking little raincoat you are wearing, you will never get a job." After a moment she added, "And when you are working, you will reimburse me."

The next morning we went to FREI in Offenbach to look for a coat. It was the biggest department store in town, and they had just what Jacques needed: a beautiful, to-the-knee, beige camel coat for DM 99. When we came home, my grandmother looked at him and said, "Don't you look handsome? And so distinguished. Now somebody will want you!"

And she was right. The next interview was with Schramm Lack und Farbenfabrik near Buergel. They hired him, and he worked in their laboratory for the next year.

"You are just like your grandmother," my mother told me often when I grew up, and even later in life. I was never sure if it was a compliment, because she did not approve of her mother in many ways. But *peu importe* since I loved and admired my grandmother, I am grateful to be like her.

The world of today marginalizes older people, and the only way to curtail this is to be friendly and understanding, using our smile to change the odds.

Retiring from Life
Is Not an Option

*Y*es, you are slowing down. Yes, you get tired more easily. And yes, you have to pace yourself, but that does not mean you have to give up on life. You just have to be more careful.

Remember to hold handrails wherever they are, leave a light on to avoid falling over something when you get up in the middle of the night, and most important, learn to appreciate the luxury of your extra free time, which will allow you to enjoy life in a new way.

Everything is relative, and how you approach the years ahead is really a matter of your perception of life, yourself, and the world around you.

Joyce and I were having lunch in a restaurant located in midtown Manhattan, a mecca for business men and young executives. We arrived at noon, and thirty minutes later, every seat around us was taken by those who have just an hour for lunch. They all ate and disappeared quickly, and we were still sitting there at 1:45 p.m. Watching this hasty coming, eating, and going-back-to-work scene was one of those moments when being elderly felt quite good.

Whoever said, "You are only as old as you feel," knew what he or she was talking about.

What does a number mean? Quite a bit, if you let it. But in truth, it is only important in your passport. In your mind, there is no place for it. How can we prevent a number from settling in? Don't ruminate over old thoughts. Avoid conversations about age, and avoid speaking solely about illness. (I have friends whose phone calls I dread because all they talk about is who is sick.)

Instead, stay active, and open your mind to new challenges, new adventures, and new people. By doing so, you will forget how old you are. By embracing the surrounding world, you will become a part of it again, instead of feeling misunderstood or left behind.

The other day at Bottomless Closet, where I volunteer, a lady who is also a volunteer asked me, "Do you know that I am eighty-five years old?"

It took me a few moments to answer.

"That's hard to believe," I said. "You are amazing."

Her hair is silver-gray, well cut, and shiny. She is always nicely dressed, and she walks with a straight back and her head held high. Volunteering only one day a week for a few hours is enough to keep her connected and make her feel useful.

Michelle, a vendor on the Seventy-Ninth Street Flea Market, has been there for many years. I was happy to see her when I visited the market a few weeks ago.

"You are still here. How nice!" I said. "How are you?"

"Well, business is not very good, but fortunately most of my merchandise is given to me on consignment, so it doesn't matter so much if I sell it or not."

As I looked over the items on her table, she came close to me and continued in a low voice, "You know I am not doing this for the money. I am doing this to have something to look forward to every Sunday, because at ninety-two, what else could I do to be in contact with people?"

"I think you are wonderful," I said, smiling at her with admiration. I added, "Where there is a will, there is a way!"

"You bet!" she said as she squeezed my hand.

Don't Let Age Be Your Excuse

Don't play the age game! Don't blame the years for the things you don't want to do. You don't need an excuse for not wanting to walk all the way downtown when you prefer taking a bus. It is like the women who blame their husbands when they don't want something—*"Oh, my husband wouldn't want that!"*—even though he was never asked.

During my recent trip to Munich, Germany, with Marc and his family, we planned to visit *Englischer Garten* (English Garden), a park in the center of the city. Before leaving the hotel, my son said, "Don't forget to put your swimsuit on under your clothes."

Before I could ask why, he was gone. When we came to the park, and we stood in front of the wild, rushing waters of the *Eisbach* (ice brook), I understood. People went there to swim. I watched as groups of young men were pushed along by the strong current; they held their beer bottles up high in the air to avoid the water spoiling their beer. (Yes, this was Germany; there is beer everywhere.)

"Oh, the water is ice cold," Marc said, shivering as he came out of the stream.

"Why don't you come in?" Ann encouraged me.

"Me? No, I don't feel like it. I don't like cold water and the strong currents."

"Really? But it's fun," she said. For a moment, I was tempted. I didn't want to look like I couldn't do it or was afraid. After considering it further, I remembered that even twenty years ago, I wouldn't have jumped in. I was never very sporty.

"A shame," Ann called out as she was carried downstream and out of sight.

Blaming how old you are as a reason for not doing something is unfair. If you think back, you will probably remember you never liked camping, and not wanting to do it now is not your age talking. It is your choice, just like it would have been twenty years earlier.

You were young longer than you will be old. Your past has taught you many lessons you can be proud of. Sometimes the online generation questions the value of your experiences because they think those are outdated, and maybe they *are* antiquated compared to the Internet, iPods, and iPhones. Yet those life experiences have made you who you are today, and you should be proud of the world you helped to create for them.

Yes, the world has changed, and one of the positive changes is that we now live much longer than ever before. But living longer has also brought about a new challenge that earlier generations never had to face.

What Comes Next?

It is a question that will be facing many of us, and it is not easy to answer, but the key here is to stay involved with the world. Never say, *"At my age."* If you feel old, it is a sign that something has to change. You must not allow this feeling to settle in, or it will paralyze you.

You may not have as many choices open to you now as you did before, but there are options that can give you a sense of purpose and enjoyment. Here are just a few activities that will help you stay connected:

- going to church
- volunteering
- enjoying museums
- attending lectures
- going to the movies and theatre

- shopping
- walking in the park
- visiting a library
- starting a new hobby
- traveling

The best thing you can do for yourself is to stay in close contact with your friends and family.

Your family probably needs you most. With your help, no strangers will be needed to babysit, no latchkey kids will be running around, and no cameras will be installed to watch the nanny at home. Unfortunately, many grandparents today see their grandchildren mostly through Skype or FaceTime, which is a wonderful option when we live a distance away, but unfortunately no one has yet found a way to let us feel our grandchildren's little arms hugging us.

Maybe everybody, young and old, should step back in time and help to recreate the bond of the family again. The contract between the generations needs renegotiating, not ditching!

In your group of friends, you need to have some young people. When I asked my friend Diana why she had joined a certain organization, she said, "I feel good going there; it makes me feel younger because everybody there is older than I."

This is not the way to go.

I am happy to say that I have friends who are half my age. Their friendship brings a new dimension to my world. When they tell me about their work or the man they just met, or we talk about the latest fashion trends, it is rejuvenating.

"*Do you know what I like about you, Rachel? You're old, like me.*"

When I was young, I never thought that one day I would not be young anymore. I was not listening when my grandmother said, "The only good thing about getting old is that it happens to everybody."

Many years later, I am still not listening. I don't feel old because I don't think I'm old. If you ask me when I will be ready to be old, my answer is—*never!*

Writing the Next Chapter of Your Life

When you speak about yourself, you always say, "In my life." But do you really have only one life? I don't think so. Looking back, I see that I went through many different phases, which all had a distinct beginning and end like chapters in a book. This phase of your life is a new chapter. Will it be a happy one filled with challenges, new experiences, joy, and laughter?

That depends on you. You are the author of this new chapter in your life, and you will write the story's happy ending. Yes, there will be difficulties, and you will have to deal with them, but the story will be happier and easier to write if you stay optimistic, positive, and refuse to let old age creep in between the lines.

The only thing constant is change. How you deal with change determines your future—and if you *never give up,* the future will be brighter!

Acknowledgments

When we look at a book and read the author's name, we see one person . . . but to write a book takes many talented professionals, and it is those special people I want to thank for all their support and help; without them this book would not have been published.

Meredith Bernstein, my friend and the agent for my previous books, never loses her enthusiasm and clear vision of what direction a book should take to be successful. When searching for a title of this book, we considered many options. Finally, it was Meredith who suggested *Getting Over Growing Older*—and I will never get over Meredith encouraging me to write another book.

What would I have done without my editor, Candace Johnson of Change It Up Editing? She helped me streamline my thoughts and put my not-so-American English into the words of the land. I am grateful for her gentle guidance, for being aware of a writer's fragile ego, and for making the path to completion a joyful and exciting experience. These are things I will always remember and be grateful for.

Thank you, Gary! Gary Rosenberg of The Book Couple is the man responsible for giving life to the parts and pieces by transforming them into a beautiful, appealing book and making it a reality. It was only when I saw the first cover layouts that I could believe I had written a book—what a thrill!

Then there was Manny Parks from Pro-Image, who

helped me (with the assistance of Ann Stenson) overcome my apprehension about a photo shot. Despite the camera's critical eye, he took a nice photo that didn't need retouching, and allows my readers to meet me while looking at the book.

My appreciation also goes to the many people I have mentioned in this book. They were—they are—part of my life, and I am grateful for their friendship. Sometimes I have changed their names, but many asked me to use their real ones, and I am happy that they wanted to be part of this journey.

And then there is my family: my daughter-in-law, Ann, my grandchildren, Remy and Cosette, and Jacques, who has been a good friend throughout my life. I thank them all for, in their own ways, making my life happier and giving it a special meaning.

Finally, I say *thank you* to my son, Marc. His patience with his less-than-computer-savvy mother made my task so much easier. He was always available and ready to help when I lost a file or didn't understand the online editing process—but in addition to his expertise with computers, I thank him for his love, and I want to tell him *"Ich lieb Dich auch! Herzlichen Dank."*

> *Alone we can do little,*
> *Together we can do so much.*
> —HELEN KELLER

Thank you, everybody!

About the Author

Drawing from her experiences as a designer, model, and owner of a design studio, as well as her connection to the fashion world in New York for many years, Brigitte Nioche wrote *Getting Over Growing Older* to encourage women to stay positive and never to give up on life—and to realize how much responsibility lies with each of us for our looks, self-confidence, and well being.

Brigitte is the author of *The Sensual Dresser, Dress to Impress,* and *What Turns Men On.* Born in Germany, she lived in Australia and Europe before moving to the United States. She is a long-time resident of New York City and a proud mother and doting grandmother who plans to never "grow old."

Learn more at www.gettingovergrowingolder.com.